THE JOURNEY

THE JOURNEY

JAYANTA BANERJEE

Copyright © 2023 by Jayanta Banerjee.

Library of Congress Control Number:		2023900589
ISBN:	Hardcover	978-1-5065-4961-3
	Softcover	978-1-5065-4960-6
	eBook	978-1-5065-4962-0

All rights reserved. No part of this book may be reproduced or transmitted in any form or by any means, electronic or mechanical, including photocopying, recording, or by any information storage and retrieval system, without permission in writing from the copyright owner.

The views expressed in this work are solely those of the author and do not necessarily reflect the views of the publisher, and the publisher hereby disclaims any responsibility for them.

Any people depicted in stock imagery provided by Getty Images are models, and such images are being used for illustrative purposes only. Certain stock imagery © Getty Images.

Print information available on the last page.

Rev. date: 19/01/2023

To order additional copies of this book, contact:
Palibrio
1663 Liberty Drive, Suite 200
Bloomington, IN 47403
Toll Free from the U.S.A 877.407.5847
Toll Free from Mexico 01.800.288.2243
Toll Free from Spain 900.866.949
From other International locations +1.812.671.9757
Fax: 01.812.355.1576
ventas@palibrio.com
849686

IN MEMORIUM

In loving memory of my grandmother
KRISHNA-MANINI DEVI

CONTENTS

Acknowledgements ix

1   Early Education 1
2   Professional Education and Training 26
3   Graduate Studies At Waterloo 66
4   Latin America 83

Postscript 217
Las Semblanazas 219

ACKNOWLEDGEMENTS

My sincere thanks to my daughter, Dr. Anyana Banerjee, for revising and editing the final draft.

Also, I am very thankful to my wife, Matilde Muñiz Troche (Matty), for her understanding and patience, while I was busy in word-processing and editing the manuscript.

Finally, I am ever grateful my ex-wife, Eligia Briceno, for taking so good care of our children and educating them during their adolescent years.

1

EARLY EDUCATION

I still remember with crystal clarity my first admission day in primary school. Yes, the school was very well known in the neighborhood and so, they had an admission test even for the kids. I was entering grade 3. My mother did the homeschooling for the first two grades and prepared me well for the third grade. I was sitting in a large room with many other kids who also applied for admission. I was looking around, full of curiosity with surprising eyes, and saw at a distance an elderly person sitting in front of a large table and talking to a little boy in front of him. It immediately occurred to me that the elderly person must be a teacher, and hence must be asking a lot of tough questions of the poor little boy.

Soon, my turn came. I approached the table and man with fear but the elderly man gave me a broad smile and said, "please sit down, my son!" This *'my son!'* totally took away my fear and I felt very relaxed. He asked, again with a smile, "How are you feeling today?" "Good, Sir." I replied, with my head a bit bent down for not looking straight in his eyes. "What did you read this morning?" he asked. I replied, this time looking straight at him, "A poem, Sir.". "Great! Can you recite it for me, my son?" This second time *'my son'* gave me a wave of joy, and I recited the full poem that my mom taught me the night before. When I finished, he was overjoyed. He stood up from his chair, and looked at me, again with a smile, and said, "You are all set for Grade 3! Come to school next Monday. Oh, by the way, bring with you a small exercise book for writing and, of course, a pencil." Apparently, I must have had my happiness reflected on my face, for he moved forward and gave me a little pat on the shoulder, and said, "Now go home and enjoy the day!" I turned around and left that large room. My father was waiting outside the door.

Later, after many months in Grade 3, I came to know why the entrance examiner was so happy with my reciting the poem. That very poem was in the textbook for Grade 3! He took me as an 'advanced student' for the class!

The school was only a five-minute walk from our house. Just across the road there was a park, and the school was located right beside the park. I could go to that very prestigious school only for its proximity! The name of the school was Mitra Institution where many famous Indians, from musicians to politicians, attended during British rule and, also after independence. Freedom fighter like Shyma Prasad Mukherjee, musicians like Hemant Kumar, went to that school. India gained freedom in 1947, and in the same year I started in Grade 3. I was only seven. It was a glorious year in Indian history and a year for me to remember at the onset of my formal education!

Homeschooling with my mother was great. There was no fixed time, no big schedule. Whenever she had time after house-spousing her daily duties she would sit with me, and we would start together reading, writing and a bit of arithmetic. She taught me the very basic addition, subtraction, multiplication, and division. We used to sing together *the multiplication table* in Bengali. It was an ideal mentor – mentee relationship!

As the classes started on a Monday, I remember I had to get up early, prepare myself to get ready, eat breakfast and reach the school gate on time. A new routine! Mother used to prepare a small lunch, and I used to take it with me in a "tiffin carrier", as was its popular name back in those years. From free homeschooling to a very scheduled school day was my first impression on how a long formal education would be waiting for me! There was a gatekeeper at the school entrance, and he would greet each schoolboy at the gate. He used to sharpen our pencils with a small knife. He was very fast in this job as we used to have a big line behind him to resharpen our dull pencils. During the recess period around lunch hour, he used to be really alerted at the gate so that no boy could sneak out of the gate and cross the street. That was a true gatekeeping duty.

The school building was quite big with four floors and a large rectangular open yard in the middle. The yard was used for sports activities, and for any large-scale gathering of the students and their teachers. Our grade 3 class was in a small room at a corner of the yard. On the same floor there were a couple of rooms, one for the gatekeeper and the other one was for a teacher. Both lived on campus.

Our classroom was good enough to accommodate roughly twenty boys. By the way, it was not a co-ed school; the girls had a separate school nearby. In our classroom, we used to share long wooden benches with attached desks, and the teacher had his own separate table and chair right in front of us.

Our class teacher was a middle-aged man in his fifties, and he had long grayish hair covering the ears and the forehead. In the very first week, he drew on the blackboard a square quadrant, just like a monthly calendar page. Then he wrote the days of the week, Monday to Friday, at the top of the horizontal rows and the hours of the day (9am – 10am, 10am -11am, 11am – lunch break, etc.) on the left end of the vertical columns. Then he wrote in each square box the subject to be taught, like English, Bengali, Arithmetic, General Knowledge, and so on. I was very confused. Yes, I remember even today that it took me quite a few days to understand the table. At home mom taught me all these things without such a complicated diagram! Again, I reflected on what a formal education would be awaiting me!

Unlike today, in those days back in 1947 we didn't have "Workbooks"; only the textbooks, an exercise book with ruled lines and a sharp pencil to write with, were good enough for early education. In the first week, the teacher handed over to us a small list of a few textbooks, mainly for Arithmetic, English, Bengali, as well as for History and Geography as a part of general knowledge. I handed over the little list to my dad. Next week when dad bought the few books and brought them home, I was surprised. He handed over the packet to me, and said softly with his usual smile, "Open the packet carefully!". I opened the packet very carefully, as he said, without tearing it apart, and there flashed out the beautifully colored cover page of each book. The living aroma of a brand-new book! I smelled each book repeatedly. This was quite a new experience! In mom's homeschooling there was no such fresh smell of a new book. I only knew the crude odor of the daily newspaper delivered at our door each early morning by the mailman.

Besides my mother, another person in our home who made a profound impact in my early childhood, and later in my education up until the university years, was my paternal grandmother. She lived with us, or in other words, we lived in her house! We, all her grandchildren, used to call her *Ma*, meaning mother in many Indo-Persian languages including our native tongue, Bengali. She was the 'beloved mother' for all her children, grandchildren, and great-grandchildren! Just one word *Ma* closed all the generation gaps.

As far as my earliest memory goes, maybe when I was 3 or 4 years old, I used to hang around a lot with my grandma. She would take me with her whenever she would go out to see her brothers and sisters and especially her nieces. Traveling with her stopped as soon as my primary school started! This was another impact that I still remember, apart from leaving my mother's homeschooling, in the earliest part of my formal education. Even today my grandma comes quite often in my dreams.

Ma took care of my school fees. It was only 7 Indian Rupees (INR) per month in those years till I finished Grade 10 in the same Mitra Institution. Like the British Matriculation system, at the end of the 10th Grade, there used to be a big State-wide exam. The city of Calcutta now renamed *Kolkata*, where I grew up, belonged to the State of West Bengal, one of the most populous and crowded states of India. So, the entrance examination to a college was long and tough. Anything could be asked from anywhere in the written tests. When I passed that exam and entered the Presidency College, another prestigious institution, my grandma continued to take care of my college fees. Her only income was the monthly rent she collected from another adjacent small house.

As I couldn't go out with my grandma any more during the week, she would sometimes postpone her visits till the weekend, and take me with her. This way I came to know some of our distant relatives. Such occasional weekend family visits with my grandma continued till I finished my college years. This way I came to know that some of my college friends were also my distant relatives. One of them, Rabin Chatterjee who lives now in Toronto, Canada, is also my distant cousin. Such family ties that built in our mind a sense of togetherness, is unfortunately lost in the modern day "modular" living system.

I have pictures with my grandmother that I share today with my children and grandchildren just to show that this extended chain of family clanship is not that bad at all. It gives a feeling of belonging to a much wider world. It makes you take the first step for a global family, a universal brotherhood. As we face today the common crisis of COVID-19, we feel the urgent need of a sincere global response, independent of the political differences and often rivalry amongst the nations, especially among the strongest ones. It can only happen if we cultivate global awareness by living in an environment where we can share our personal belongings with others. From this point of view, a "joint family" environment has much to contribute. I knew a family where four brothers lived together in a big ancestral house. They all had different jobs in the same city. Family expenses were shared proportionately according to their individual monthly incomes. But the most impressive sight was that all of them and their wives and children would share the same kitchen and enjoy the same evening meal after returning home from work and from school. This way the cousins shared things like brothers and sisters!

In the 1960s the hippies experienced sharing things in the environment of a common family in their communal living.

During the Vietnam War, many young hippies left the USA and moved North to Canada to avoid the compulsory military "draft "of the USA. They were also ridiculed and searched worldwide by the US government as *"Draft Dodgers"*! I had the opportunity to live a few months with them in Northern Ontario, Canada. They not only lived together in a commune but also worked together in harmony throughout the day. In the evening we would all eat together the same food cooked by the women, and then we used to sing together before going to bed. It was a wonderful lesson of love and peace! There was no difference in daily food and shelter, no matter whether you were a millionaire's daughter from California or a poor farmer's son from Maine. We were all *Draft Dodgers*, as if war criminals, in the eyes of the US government authorities! While with the hippies, I used to remember the communal family system amongst some of my relatives in India many years ago. Even with the difference of diverse cultures between the modern hippies and that of ancient India, both worked well. With the mounting problems of today: COVID-19, Global Warming from pollution, increasing population particularly in the poorer parts of the world and, above all, the extreme misunderstanding and economic war amongst the superpowers, such as between bigger and stronger Russia and relatively smaller and weaker Ukraine, a sense of fellow-feeling in the younger generations is a viable solution for harmonizing our future existence on this perturbed planet Earth.

Summer vacations were long for the hot and humid months, from May to July, in Bengal. In one such vacation, grandma took me with her to one of her daughters' homes in the beautiful city of Shillong, situated at the foothills of the Eastern Himalayas. This was my first experience in the mountains. My auntie's house was near the top of a hilly section of the city, called *Mulky*. We had to move up a winding path with many stone steps in between to reach our home, walking from the city center where the main shopping areas were located. I used to accompany my auntie's husband to buy groceries downtown, and on the way back it was a very good exercise climbing up a few hundred steps on a winding path. He would usually carry the big shopping bag on his back, and I would carry the smaller one. On the way up he used to tell me many stories of his living experience in Shillong and about the tribal people who initially settled there long before the people from Bengal and Assam moved into this mountainous region during the British regime that continued for almost two centuries.

Three hilly tribes, namely, *Bhutia, Khashia* and *Jayantia*, lived in and around the city of Shillong. They were the original settlers in that eastern end of the Himalayan range that bordered with Nepal and China. Shillong was the biggest city of the province of Assam, adjacent to West Bengal. The state language of Assam is *Assamese*, similar to *Bengali* or *Bangla* in its scripts, but quite different in speaking. Besides, the three hilly tribes have their own dialects. Most of the tribal people were Christianized by the local missionary groups but they all lived in harmony with others, mainly with the Hindus and the Muslims. My auntie's next-door neighbor was a Khashia family; they were Christians, and very good friends of my auntie's family. These tribal societies were matriarchal, meaning the lady of the family was the biggest boss. The head of our neighbor's family was a fine lady in her late fifties or early sixties; and we used to call her *mammy*. My two cousins: *Manju* and *Khokon*, a girl and a boy respectively, were very much attached to mammy. She used to give them a lot of

Indian sweets and sometimes imported chocolate candies as well. She had several girls and only one boy, *Mike*. The girls also had all Christian names, like *Nancy, Susan,* etc., and Christan education. While leading a Christian way of life, like going to the church every Sunday, they respected the local Hindu and Muslim customs. At that time Mike was around 25; and he used to smoke cigarettes. In Christian customs there is nothing wrong with smoking publicly in front of others, but in the Hindu customs, younger people don't smoke in front of the elderly persons. Every time Mike would see my auntie's husband, he would hide his cigarette!

I was around 12 years old then. My cousin Manju was 9 and her little brother, Khokon was 5. Manju and I used to hang around each other a lot, sometimes playing, sometimes fighting over petty things, like who would accompany auntie to pick up the pieces of wood for burning in the chimney at night, or who would stay home with grandma to help her cut vegetables. Khokon was too small to do any of those household jobs.

The Khashias had their traditional tribal festivities along with the Christian festivals. One of them was a very colorful folk-dance festival only once a year. It used to take place in a village called *Nongcraime,* at the outskirts of Shillong. My auntie's husband once took us there. The dresses were so colorful, and the rhythmic steps were so fast that Manju and I were surprised. Khokon was spell-bound! The steps were as fast as the modern *salsa* or *merengue* in the Caribbean part of Latin America. Various groups from different villages participated in that grand gala that lasted for several hours each evening under the canopy of a full-moon sky!

That was my first trip to an area so different from the big city of Calcutta! As the summer vacation was coming close to its end in the last week of July, huge Monsoon rain attacked Shillong and the whole province of Assam was under water! There were great floods all over in the planes of Assam, and the rail-lines for the passenger and goods trains were all shattered. There was no train connection because of the derailment. We couldn't afford to pay airfare. So, my grandma and I were stuck in Shillong for several months!

We used to have a lot of homework in summer for the class. Since I was stuck in Shillong for the whole summer and further into August-September, a classmate of mine helped me with finishing my homework until the rails were repaired and we could get back to Kolkata. His name was *Bachchu* and was a good friend of mine and a close neighbor. He helped me in math and handwriting. He was very good at math. In those days there were no laptops, and we had to do everything by hand. Therefore, the handwriting exercises were very important, almost like practicing calligraphy!

Bachchu's family lived on the same street as ours, only a couple of houses ahead. The street was very narrow, almost a lane, and a wider car couldn't pass through. We were all neighborhood kids and used to hang around together. Apart from the park across the wider road, there was a smaller playground on the other side of the lane, and we used to play there barefoot soccer in summer and wicket-less cricket in winter. There was also a slum nearby. We were used to all standards of living, mainly the middle-class and lower middle class. Extreme poverty of Kolkata was not around us, not even in our nearby slums. The culture of sharing things among the neighbors helped reducing extreme poverty in the families and its crude picture was unseen in our neighborhood. As a child, I could only remember a very impressive but sad scene of poverty, and that was a beggar in all torn out filthy clothes crawling in the middle of that narrow lane and all the passers-by were looking at him in disgust. He couldn't hold his body in balance even while crawling; his skin was full of leprosy-like rashes. He was really in a miserable condition! The scene was so strong that I still remember it even after some 75+ years!

The other end of the lane ended where *Hooghly* River, a small territory of the famous *Ganges* or Ganga of India, flowed through the subcontinent. It was about 1000 ft from our house. As kids we learned swimming in that river. We didn't need a swimming pool! The river was a very intimate part of my childhood memories. Small boats used to anchor at its bank for supplying house construction materials, mainly sand, bricks, cement, etc. to the local industries. We, the neighborhood kids, would often jump on those boats, play there, and watch the boatmen smoking their favorite waterpipes, called *hukkahs*, and relaxing with their usual gossip at the time of sunset. They never asked us to get out!

Three neighborhood kids were my friends: *Moni, Dipu* and *Dulal*. They are all gone now but the childhood memories are still vivid. We used to play barefoot soccer in that small playground near our house. The usual practice hours were from 4pm till the sunset, depending upon the season of the year. In summer we had long hours to play almost till 7PM, but in winter the sun sets much earlier and at six it was already dark! Very often we would get *hell* from our parents for returning so late after the sunset!

My best friend was Moni. We two used to hang around each other all the time after school hours. When we became a bit bigger, we wanted to learn how to ride a bike. There was no bicycle around except one of Moni's uncles had one that he used for going to his work during the week. One Sunday afternoon when he was doing his *siesta* at home, Moni and I silently and very carefully took his bike out and took it to the bigger park across the road. We tried to jump on it, and after quite a few tries we could balance and ride on it. What a delight! From that day on, every Sunday two of us used to take that bike out very silently while his uncle would be sleeping.

One afternoon something serious happened. While riding the bike in the park, I had to use the handbrake very abruptly and fast because suddenly I saw an old woman on my way crossing the track. I fell and the handle of the bike hit hard on the ground and got twisted. We both got very upset: How to fix it before taking it back home? We tried hard to straighten it out, but we were not strong enough to twist it back to its initial position. Finally, an older boy came and fixed it. What a relief from the fear of being beaten by Moni's uncle!

I think we were around ten years old during that period. There were many festivities once the very hot and humid summer of Kolkata and the heavily affecting Monsoon rain were gone by late August or early September. The first one was *Durga Puja,* the largest of all the festivals and it lasted for 5 to 6 days. The entire city used to be full of joy and merriment forgetting all the miseries of the year around the calamities of a monstrous metropolis! It was like the Carnival in Rio de Janeiro. People were full of joy!

This was the time of the year when we, the kids, used to get new clothes and shoes only once a year and would eagerly wait to get them and try them out right away. Family visits were very common as it was a vacation time. Many times our aunties came and stayed with us. The house was full of people and full of joy even with our limited family resources. One doesn't have to be rich to enjoy the simple things of life! In the big park, (called Harish Park, named after a patriot and freedom fighter Harish Mukherjee), the elder members of our community used to construct a huge and very spacious covered tent-like structure for the *Durga Pratima,* a statue of Durga and her family as per Hindu mythology, and for people to get around. There used to be many stalls selling things from warm food, cold drinks to all kinds of toys for the kids. During those five to six days, the kids used to spend most of the time in the park, eating fried peanuts with onion, drinking all kinds of fresh fruit juice or a variety of lemonades, and playing barefoot soccer. Our parents used to go out in a small group, mainly in the evening. Durga Puja in Kolkata was full of festivities and family gatherings every year.

Within a month after Durga Puja comes Kali Puja, usually in October or November. *Ma Kali* is the goddess of strength, and she arrives on earth alone, not with the entire family like *Ma Durga*. Kali Puja's duration was usually two days but also with full of enthusiasm all over Kolkata because of the fireworks at night. Pyro- activities, such as making different types of fireworks and then shooting them into the night sky, were a thrill for the older kids while we the younger kids had our hand-held small fireworks. Even the elders, like my father and uncles and their friends, enjoyed making fireworks with different combinations of mixtures of aluminum and gun powders for making those fireworks and then shooting them high in the sky at night. It was like flying a kite in India where even very old people are crazily passionate about it! I remember my dad and his friends were all excited about flying kites even in their sixties and seventies.

Between Durga Puja and Kali Puja, about five days after the end of Durga Puja *(Vijaya Dashami* or *Dasha Hara)* we had a small *Lakshmi Puja*. *Ma Lakshmi* is the goddess of wealth and fortune, even though the puja was not celebrated so gorgeously as Durga and Kali pujas. After Kali puja, the festivities continued with several other pujas of smaller dimensions, like *Jagat-dhatri puja, Kartik puja,* etc. Thus, a series of pujas of greater and smaller festivities in a series of gods and goddesses used to extend till December. Then comes in January another big Puja: *Saraswathi Puja. Ma Saraswathi is* the goddess of learning and music. She plays *Vina,* a string instrument much more complicated than our guitar. The great importance of Saraswathi puja in schools and colleges was for praying to enhance our progress in studies, such as the grades in exams, no matter in primary school or in postdoc research. It was a good occasion to meet the alumni and get around with the new students and teachers. It used to be more of a social get together than a religious festival.

In later years, when I went to Jadavpur University to study Engineering, there was one professor in our Mechanical Engineering department who also happened to attend the same Primary and Secondary school, Mitra Institution, where I went. Thus, during Saraswathi puja on the school campus, we used to meet and talk to him in a more relaxed and closer environment which eventually helped me in scoring good grades under his guidance. His name was Bibhu Mukherjee, and he was a professor of Fluid Mechanics. He was one of the smartest and *chic* instructors I ever had throughout my student years including my graduate studies at Waterloo University and Queens University in Canada. We used to call him Bibhu *Babu*, as a mark of respect in our Indian culture. Bibhu Babu used to give his class lectures without looking at his class notes, and his drawings on the blackboard with a simple piece of a white chalk were impeccable. Remember, I am talking about the years of the mid-fifties when there were no computers or smartphones, not even white boards with colored markers!

Bibhu Babu used to offer another course where each student had to choose a topic and speak on the topic in front of the students, and field questions from them for an hour, just like an instructor. It was a good course to get used to public speaking, no matter if you want to be a teacher, an entrepreneur, or a manager in any industry. One student in our class was extremely good at public speaking because he was on a debating team in high school. His name was Jawaharlal Maheshwari. He was a very smart student in our class, an all-rounder! Bibhu Babu used to tease him sometimes, calling him "Prime Minister", because during those years, the first Prime Minister of independent India was Jawaharlal Nehru, father of our famous Indian "Iron lady", Indira Gandhi, who was also another Prime Minister of India in later years. Indira Gandhi was compared with another iron lady, Margaret Thatcher of the UK.

This public speaking course helped me a lot in the future while working in other countries. In the beginning, I was a bit shy type, but this course got me out of fear of talking to people at large scale gatherings, such as teaching a class at a university, a profession that I pursued for most of my life. For example, when I first came to teach in Latin America, I was very nervous to start my lecture in Spanish, a language that I just learned a bit through a three-months crash course in Cuernavaca, Mexico. In my first lecture I was dumb-stuck! There, in front of some thirty students, Bibhu Babu's image came up suddenly after so many years, and I got the spirit of speaking in front of strange faces in a new language that I just started to learn. This was at the University *Del Valle* in Cali, Colombia in early 1970. I also got a lot of help from my Colombian colleagues in preparing and translating my class notes from English to Spanish. I will talk about that later.

In 1947, after the partition of India and Pakistan, many Hindu Bengalis migrated from East Bengal or East Pakistan (now Bangladesh) to Calcutta (now Kolkata), and many new teachers from East Bengal joined our school, Mitra Institution. We were very lucky to have many talented teachers with a lot of experience, who unfortunately had to migrate from East Bengal. They spoke Bengali with a different accent initially but quickly picked up our Calcutta dialect. We also had many young teachers who used to come temporarily as a part of their practice in their Bachelor of teaching (BT) courses. This way, we the students benefited by being exposed to a variety of instructors and their ways of teaching.

I stayed in Mitra Institution from 1947 till finishing grade 10 in 1955, and then moved to Presidency College where my great-grandfather and grandfather were also students. Both were lawyers, and my great-grandfather became a District Judge in Bihar province during the British rule in India. That was a prestigious position for a "colored native Indian" in a British colony! My change in basic education from a high school to a college, especially to the highly traditional Presidency College, was a great transition. The college had some of the best professors of Calcutta University. This is the same college where Professor C. V. Raman did his famous experiment of "Raman Effect "in Optics that later fetched him a Nobel Prize in Physics in 1931, and made his work recognized worldwide. It is the same institution where Professor P. C. Mahalanabish of Statistics founded his international journal, *Sankhya*. We were lucky to have professors like P. C. Sen of Chemistry, author of a great textbook, and Professor Shivatosh Mukherjee (grandson of Sir Ashutosh Mukherjee, the Tiger of Bengal!) in Biology and Professor Sushavan Sirkar in History! Presidency College was indeed a great fountain of inspiration for us, the beginners aspiring to get into a professional career in medicine, law, literature, science, or engineering. It had excellent libraries as well as many sports facilities including soccer and cricket.

We had two years of preparation at Presidency, equivalent to Grades 11 and 12 in the US and Canadian systems. In Math, we had differential and integral calculus and some basic differential equations up to the second order. In Physics, we had heat, light, sound, electricity, magnetism, and general physics including gravity and gravitational field. We also had statics in the first year and dynamics in the second year. In Biology we had one year of Zoology and one year of Botany. Besides, we had in humanities courses, English and Bengali as languages as well as history, economics, sociology, etc. as optional choices, not compulsory. In science we had several options of geology, physiology, anthropology, and many others. In fact, those two years at Presidency were very intensive but built the foundation stone of preparation for entering a university level education, no matter whether it was in engineering, medicine, arts, and humanities.

I got interested in literature, attracted by the class lectures of some of the very dynamic instructors in Bengali and English at Presidency. But in those years of the mid-fifties the trend was in engineering, and many of my very close friends from Mitra Institution and Presidency College were going to take engineering. So, I decided to follow my buddies so as to not lose touch with them. Some of them were my buddies since Grade 3, and I couldn't think of spending my time without them. I applied for admission only at Jadavpur University in the Engineering faculty. That was the only engineering school where I could attend my classes while staying at home and thus getting a bachelor's degree after some four years.

I couldn't afford financially to go to a residential college, such as Bengal Engineering (BE) College in Sibpur, or Indian Institute of Technology (IIT) in Khargpur. Both were close enough to Kolkata. But I didn't apply there; I couldn't afford it!

When the letter of interview for admission came from Jadavpur University, I was very excited and yet very skeptical. Glad, because I was at least selected for an interview based on my grades at Presidency; skeptical, because my heart was still in literature! I applied in engineering not just for hanging around with my pals but also for some financial security after graduation in four years. I wanted a better economic stability in my future than in my past. Mechanical engineering was in great demand those days for job security, especially in those big plants in Durgapur, Raurkela, Vilai, etc. that India was building with full force after its independence from the British empire, not just political and economic freedom but also to get out of the curse of cultural colonialism.

On the day of my interview, I reached the Jadavpur campus on time and, fortunately, didn't feel nervous at all. I was waiting outside the Rector's office, the venue of my future career, but didn't find any of my pals around. They were probably called for an interview at a different date, and I had no chance to ask them what they were asked during their interviews. Anyway, as the door opened and I was called inside, I found a galaxy of some six or seven professors sitting in a row in front of a long and narrow elliptical desk-like table. I sat on a chair in front of them, facing Dr. *Triguna Sen*, the Rector, right in front of me. They all looked friendly and greeted me with welcoming smiles. There were some basic technical questions on math and physics from each of them. I don't remember them today after some 65 years. It was the year of 1957 when the Lebanon crisis was going on in full throttle in the Middle East. I read the newspaper that morning before leaving home for my interview. Rector Sen, sitting in front of me, asked me the final question on the current Lebanon crisis. I don't remember exactly what the question was, but I answered it to Dr. Sen's satisfaction, as he nodded his head affirmatively several times, and then smiled. All of them congratulated me and asked me to leave the room. As I left the room, I was almost sure that I would be admitted. In a few days a letter, stamped with the logo of Jadavpur University, arrived in the mailbox. I opened it with nervousness and excitement. Yes, I was admitted in Mechanical Engineering!

In sum, my early education, starting from my mom's homeschooling to Grade 12 at Presidency College, was quite a living experience. In my mom's teaching the hours were flexible. Whenever she had time away from house-spousing, she would sit with me and recite poems from books, sing multiplication tables or teach on a scrap paper how to add and subtract, multiply and divide. That method was fantastic! I realize now after some sixty years of teaching at different universities worldwide in different languages of instruction that the flexibility and the freedom of thoughts are extremely important for developing our minds in the earliest part of our education.

Then came the routine learning in Grade 3 at Mitra Institution. It was quite a change for me from flextime to a standard class schedule of the day. The weekends were better because I could hang out with my grandma visiting her relatives, meeting new people, and seeing new places. My best company was with my grandma! In grade 5, many new teachers joined the school, especially those who came from East Bengal, now Bangladesh. Their children also joined the school as our fellow classmates. The class panorama changed, and the classes became more interesting. After some seventy years we still stay in touch with some of those classmates of grade 5. We are scattered all over the globe, from Australia to Canada, from Japan to Latin America, but the new technologies of Smartphone, Facebook, Zooming and Google Meet have helped in keeping us close together in cyberspace.

At the end of Grade 10, we used to have a very competitive state-wise exam where students from all schools of the state of West Bengal had to sit for this exam. This was equivalent to British "Matriculation", only the name was changed to "School Final" after 1947 when the British left and India became an independent country after almost two centuries. That exam used to take place after summer vacation. So, we had about two to three months of summer in preparation for this tough test. Closer friends of the class used to get together to prepare for different courses of the written exams. No, there were no oral tests, thank goodness! Some of us used to attend private "coaching classes" offered by our own schoolteachers upon some extra payment. I couldn't afford that. So, we used to create our own peer coaching with two or three good friends like Rajen, Mrinal and Deshranjan. This partnership in preparing for exams continued till the university years, rather than studying alone. And it worked! We all passed the School Final exams with good grades in "First Division". Teamwork made the dream work! Even today I divide my class into groups of three students in each group, and most of my assignments are in groups!

During Grades 11 and 12 at Presidency College, things changed a bit, since Rajen, Mrinal and Deshranjan went to a different institution, St. Xavier's College that competed with Presidency. Both were very well-known colleges in Calcutta.

While St. Xavier's was a private institution administered by a Christian Missionary group, Presidency College was a public institution governed by the State of West Bengal and closer to the University of Calcutta. The tuition fees were also much less. Hence, I chose the Presidency. Besides the financial factor, both my paternal great-grandfather *Purnachandra* and grandfather *Kshetranath* went to the same prestigious institution, and it was kind of a family tradition and pride for me to join Presidency.

Two years at Presidency, from 1955 to 1957 were very different from my ten years of schooling at Mitra Institution. There were the students from all over the State of Bengal, the best ones, and from the other states of India. The environment was very competitive. Everyone was trying to get the best grade for getting into Medicine, Engineering, Science, or Humanities, Arts and later maybe Law school. Plus, we had very good sports facilities, debating and drama societies, music and fine arts associations as well as magazines for publishing articles and other cross-cultural activities.

Both Mitra Institution and Presidency College were very "nationalistic", particularly after 1947 when the British left India and the euphoria of nationalism skyrocketed. Nevertheless, both institutions, Presidency and St. Xavier's, produced national leaders long before India's independence and many of them, in fact, were the fighters for our freedom. For example, Presidency College produced Netaji Subhas Chandra Bose; and Mitra Institution produced Shyama Prasad Mukherjee. Rajendra Prasad, the first President of independent India, was a product of Presidency College. Not only in politics but also in science and arts these two institutions contributed a lot. Professor C. V. Raman was at Presidency where he conducted his pioneering research in optics. In modern Indian music, Hemanth Kumar was a product of Mitra Institution. I was lucky to meet him personally because he used to come to our prize distribution ceremony every year to sing his favorite songs that conquered Bollywood in Mumbai, Tollywood in Kolkata and finally, Hollywood in the US. The same was with Satyajit Ray, the famous film director who received a lifetime award in Hollywood.

We have tried to stay in touch with our school pals since 1947! We organize our get-togethers at least once a year in Kolkata with music, folkdance, poetry recitation and most importantly great food for lunch and spicy snacks after. Usually, we meet around ten in the morning, starting with tea and some snacks. Then comes lunch with all kinds of typical Bengali plates, and, of course, a variety of sweets at the end. The program continues till four in the afternoon with more tea and snacks. Some of our pals would hide a bit in the kitchen for a few shots of whisky. I just heard that this year the get together and ADDA had to be postponed till March or even later due to Omicron, the recent version of COVID-19 that is spreading furiously worldwide.

In the School Final exam in 1955, our Mitra school performed magnificently producing excellent results. Three of our group: Manoj, Hriditosh and Amitava, came 2nd, 7th and 10th respectively in a statewide exam that included a competition of several hundred thousand students! Most of us went to Presidency or St. Xavier's for the next two years leading to the Intermediate of Science, Arts or Commerce certificate that was mandatory for admission at any university, no matter in which field: science, arts, commerce, medicine, or engineering. Both Presidency and St. Xavier's were traditionally very well-established colleges. Imagine, my great grandfather was a student at Presidency and my uncles went to St. Xavier's!

In the beginning, the transition from a school to a college was not easy. In college, you don't sit in the same room all day. We had to move from room to room, from building to building to attend classes. Physics classes were in the Physics building, Biology classes in the Biology building and so on. Sometimes we had to run from one building to another when the classes were in succession without any "off period". Another thing, we had more freedom to skip class in college! In some classes there were "Roll Calls" for tabulating our attendance. Sometimes we would sneak out after the roll calls. In a big "lecture theater" with so many students in Physics or Chemistry classes, who is going to notice?

While there was more freedom, there were also more responsibilities in preparing for tests, exams and especially for Physics, Chemistry and Biology labs. We had to do it all by ourselves for the final exams. In a British system in those days, unlike the American standard tests of today, there were no quizzes, partial exams, short tests, multiple choices, or yes/no type questions. In some courses, there were "Half Yearly" exams, but the main thrust was on a final exam for each course at the end of each year. But the main exam was statewide, just like the School Final exam in 1955. There was no control of any college on such an exam. All questions were set by the Calcutta University professors, and we had no clue whatsoever on the questions to be asked in any course.

This time, in May 1957, my seat for writing all the exams was set in the Senate Hall of Calcutta University, next door to our Presidency College. I had never seen such a huge hall in my life before. Five hundred students could sit there easily. The tables and chairs were placed in the form of a matrix of rows and columns; and there was a guard at the end of each row, not just for checking if we were copying but also for any other emergency assistance. It was very well organized despite so many students writing exams in a crowded super-hall. There in the huge Senate Hall of Calcutta University, during such an exam, silence and discipline were amazing!

The last day of the exam was Biology test. All exams were for three hours of written tests. I didn't do very well in Biology. I had to leave several questions unanswered. So, I left the hall early and went to see an exhibition that was going on for weeks at the University Institute, next door to the Senate Hall. I walked a few minutes and there I was within a beautiful environment of so many pictures and paintings arranged lively in different small halls. I forgot instantly about my Biology test and the Senate Hall! The name of the exhibition was *Family of Man;* and it was traveling from city to city in India and abroad. It was in Calcutta for a few weeks, and we were lucky to see it during that period after the exams. I still remember that there were some original sketches and paintings of Satyajit Ray who later became world famous as a film director, creating the *Trilogy of Apu,* and was honored with the Life-time award from Hollywood.

When the results of the Intermediate of Science came, I found myself in the cluster of "First Division" even with my disaster in the Biology test. Thank God, it helped me for admission at Jadavpur University, for a good grade in Biology would have probably been an excuse of mine to get into Medicine!

The memories of Mitra school and Presidency College were wonderful, as pure as gold! Childhood memories were so deep that they could not be erased from our minds. I still have contacts with some of my Grade 5 pals, thanks to the modern technology of smartphones and Facebook. At Presidency we made new friendships. Two of my great friends there were Nirmal and Subas. Nirmal was my partner in Chemistry lab., and I still address him sometimes as "my partner" when we meet on Zoom video-meetings. At college we used to tease Subas as "Netaji". He used to defend himself, responding, "I'm not Subhas but Subas." And we kept teasing him: "So, you don't speak well but smell well!" (In Bengali, *Subhas* means '*speaking well* 'and *Subas* is 'smelling well'). We try to stay in touch even today!

From 1947 till 1957, these years were the budding period of our basic education. There were many anecdotes that created the foundation of our belief system. Today we admire the unselfish dedication of our primary school teachers who were not great scientists and scholars like the Nobel laureates, but who ingrained into our flourishing young minds the basic principles of honesty, ethics, discipline and hence the integrity of character building. We are so grateful to our Grade 3 teachers! The Presidency College's training was also inspiring in science. Many of our professors there were the authors of the textbooks that were prescribed for the courses we were taking. It was so inspiring to see the person in front of us in the class and at the same time turning the pages of his/her book!

2

PROFESSIONAL EDUCATION AND TRAINING

Our first year at Jadavpur was exciting! I used to take a local train from Ballygunge railway station to Jadavpur station because I had a free pass through my dad who was an Indian Railways employee. From Jadavpur train station to our university campus was a five-minute walk and the route was very scenic with fresh fruit vendors on both sides of the narrow street, full of the aroma of ripe guava, banana, and mango in their respective seasons. Sometimes I would take a bus ride by bus number 2B (I still remember the number!) from our home straight to the university campus. That was more expensive, and I used to take it only when I was running out of time to attend classes. But I enjoyed the train ride more and the nice short walk on the narrow, winding walkway of a green rural environment.

In those decades engineering curricula were all charged with technical courses. In the freshman year, we had only one socio-humanistic course, and that was English. We had a lot of fun with our English teacher because he was very humorous, a real jolly good fellow in his fifties or sixties; hard to guess his actual age because of the very lively spirit in his lectures. Other courses were mere repetition of what we already had at Presidency or any other college during our two years of Intermediate of Science courses: Statics, Dynamics, Calculus, Physics and Chemistry. That repetition was very boring!

In second or sophomore year, we saw something new that we didn't have before: Mechanics, Materials Science, Mechanisms of Machines; and they were more interesting. I call them "MMMs", the fundamentals for Mechanical Engineering. In parallel, there was also Thermodynamics that made the circuit complete in the basics of Mechanical Engineering. Thermodynamics was taught by Dr. Satish Bhattacharya, who was the author of the textbook. Dr. Bhattacharya had a Dr. Ing. Degree from the Technical University of Berlin. We used to take note of every word he spoke or wrote on the board. Dr. Bhattacharya had a special talent in numerical calculations. He would put numbers on each symbol of a long algebraic equation. Then he would look at the numbers and their symbols, like division, multiplication, square root, etc. for a few minutes and then would write the final answer up to the second decimal place, while we would be struggling with our new slide-rule type calculator of those days in order to come only to the first place of decimals. There was no pocket calculator in 1957!

Dr. Triguna Sen, our Rector and Dr. Bhattacharya's contemporary, went to the Technical University of Munich for his Doctorate Degree. Remember that when they were young high school students, India was fighting for freedom, and the tendency of the National Council of Education of Bengal was to send those bright kids to Germany or USA, rather than to the UK. That was mainly due to a well justified nationalistic feeling of the political struggle. Jadavpur University was the product of the National Council of Education that was actively supported by the heroes of Bengal like the famous poet Rabindranath Tagore, Sri Aurobindo, and many others.

At Jadavpur, I felt closer to our professors. In Freshman year when we just started, we were invited to a dinner where the Rector Dr. T. Sen, the Provost Professor Gopal Sen and many other eminent professors and research scholars sat and talked and ate with us on the same table as long-time friends! Here we felt our teachers were closer to us. That never happened at Presidency!

During those four years of undergraduate engineering education, we made great friends, some of us are still in touch through the "virtual" video chats of Zoom, Google Meets and so on, thanks to cyberspace technology. We left Jadavpur in 1961, and as I am scribbling these words in 2022, I am relishing those loving memories of my undergrad years! The world has changed in galloping steps through these six decades, for good and for bad, but our friendship has stayed intact. One of our old friends joked the other day during our video conference: There are big ships and small ships, but the best ship is friendship!

In May 1961 most of us graduated with a bachelor's degree in engineering. Then came the period of job hunting. I got an engineering trainee position, equivalent to EIT (Engineer in Training) in USA and Canada, in Remington Rand, the well-known American firm's subsidiary in India. Four of us, Dulal, Ajoy and myself of mechanical engineering and Subrata of chemical engineering joined on the same day. It was great to be together again after a few months of being out of touch! The plant was in Sibpur, on the other side of the

Ganges, separating it from Calcutta. It was not too far from Bengal Engineering College (which is now an autonomous university!) where we had a few more friends as well. For the first time a full-time well-paid job was a great feeling of financial freedom!

After eating a full breakfast of *chapati* and *dal*, I used to take the bus at 7:30 am from right in front of our home to reach the plant at 8:30 am with only one change of bus at Howrah Station, a big hub for both trains and buses. My mother used to prepare a small bag for lunch. My first boss was Mr. Chitta Ghose whose engineering education was from England. He was an extremely friendly person and didn't have any vanity of a posh British school. During the two tea breaks, at 10:30am and 2:30 pm, he used to invite me daily to have tea and snacks with him in his office.

I was in the manufacturing plant for small parts of a typing machine which was the main product of Remington Rand type machines in India. I worked hand in hand with the machine operators and tool setters and learned from them a lot on the automatic and semi-automatic machine tools, like lathe, milling machines, drills and punch presses. Thanks to our Jadavpur University's workshops, especially the *Blue Earth*, we had good practice on similar machines during our Junior and Senior (3rd and 4th) years. I must admit that our engineering curricula at Jadavpur were very solid and satisfactory, and I never felt deficient while in further training in Germany and then during the graduate studies at Waterloo in Canada.

After a couple of months, Mr. Chitta Ghose moved up quickly on the professional ladder, because of his excellent communication skills, and he became the Production Manager of the plant. He was shifted to a bigger and better office in a different section of the plant, and Mr. Chi Pu came in his place as my next boss. Mr. Chi Pu was a Chinese Indian, as much an Indian as I am! Probably his family came to Calcutta several generations ago. I had a standing invitation to enjoy our tea breaks with him just the same way as before with Mr. Chitta Ghose. There was no change, no discrimination for me being just a trainee engineer or engineering in training (EIT)! Mr. Chi Pu was a more "practical" engineer. His technical skill with the machine tools – lathe, milling machine or radial drills – was outstanding. His hands were very precise; he could sharpen a cutting tool within the thousandth of an inch of tolerance!

While working in Remington, I was also trying for a further training opportunity abroad, mainly in Germany: West Germany in those decades of cold war. There was a professor in Chemical Engineering at Jadavpur, Dr. Ram Narayan Mukherjee, who recently got back from the Technical University of Stuttgart after receiving his Dr. Ing Degree there. I met him one day at Jadavpur and frankly expressed my ambition for getting further practical training in a manufacturing plant in Germany. I have a feeling now that Dr. Ram Mukherjee was impressed by my open-minded expression at our very first meeting. He got my name and home address written on his writing pad (there were no smartphones in 1961!) and assured me that he would write on my behalf to the German Indian Association (Deutsch-Indische Gesellschaft) in Stuttgart. He was very sincere because in a month, a letter came from the same association directly to me asking me to send them a certified copy of my academic transcripts of Jadavpur. It was very exciting for me to get that letter; I still remember sending them my transcripts as soon as possible. It looked like everything was really quick in Germany, because by early December 1961, I got another letter from the same association a job offer as a "Praktikant" (trainee) in a tool and cutter grinding machine manufacturing firm in Eningen/Reutlingen, very close to Stuttgart. I was thrilled and showed the letter of appointment to my mother and grandma!

Next Monday I showed the letter to Mr. Chi Pu during our morning tea break. After glancing over the letter his eyes flashed. He got up from his chair, came around his huge executive desk to me and gave me a big hug: Congratulations, Banerjee! I could see a light of genuine delight on his face! Then he went back to his seat and told me that it was a good idea to get some training abroad, especially in a technically advanced country like Germany. He added that he wished he had a similar opportunity when he was younger. Both Mr. Chitta Ghose and Mr. Chi Pu, my two bosses at Remington, were in their mid-forties.

Before the Christmas break, I wrote a formal letter (not a letter of resignation!) to our General Manager, Mr. Deeth, stating that I would like to have a leave of absence for furthering my training abroad, and I attached a copy of the letter of appointment from the German Indian Association. Mr. Deeth wrote to me a very nice reply stating that since I was then only a few months working in Remington, the company wouldn't be able to give me a leave of absence but could release me unconditionally with the hope of reemploying me upon my return from Germany provided the conditions were satisfactory and mutually agreeable. I showed the letter to Mr. Chi Pu, and he was, as always, very happy with my preparation for progress.

After the Christmas break, I applied for the West German working visa at its Consulate in Calcutta. Since the work offer was through the German Indian Association in Stuttgart, the Visa was stamped very fast on my Indian passport that I also got quickly based on the job offer directly through the German Indian Association. This was also because the same association had close connections with the Goethe Institute in Calcutta. The entire process of getting an Indian passport and a West German visa stamped on my passport took less than a month. It was surprisingly fast considering the slow administrative and communication procedure in India in the early sixties when the country was emerging as a new nation after its independence.

Then came the question of funds for travel. I contacted a travel agent and found that traveling by passenger ship was much cheaper than airfare. Around that time there was an Italian boat coming from New Zealand and Australia, and would be touching Colombo in Sri Lanka, Cochin in South India *en route* Sicily, Milan and Genoa in Italy. I don't remember now how much my ticket costed but I was allowed to take with me a traveler's cheque of seventy British Pounds. My parents and my grandma didn't have that amount of money but my maternal grandfather and my aunt, on my mother's side, helped. The part of travel within India, from Calcutta to Cochin by train, was free since my father was a railway employee. That way I somehow managed the financial part and remained ever grateful to my mother's family. I also learned that a summation of little helps makes a big difference!

Finally, on one fine morning in February 1962 (I think it was February 12!) I left Calcutta by train to Cochin via Madras (now Chennai). My grandma came to the front door of our house and gave me a strong hug; tears rolled down her eyes. That was the last time I saw my grandma. While typing these words after some sixty years, I feel nostalgia for her. The other members of the family went with me in two taxis to the main train station in Howrah. At the train station I met some of my friends: Swapan, Rajen, Hiren and a few others. My parents and an aunt came as well with my two sisters. We took a group picture with the train as its background. (My youngest son, Nayan, inherits that memorable picture now as a family treasure!). I had very little luggage, only two small suitcases. The whistle blew, I went up and the train slowly started moving. I raised my hand to say goodbye.

In the train compartment, I met several boys of about my age who were also traveling to Germany and England on the same mission of getting industrial training. It took a couple of days till we reached Cochin with a short stop over and train change in Madras. The connections arranged by the travel agent were so good that we didn't need to stay overnight, neither in Madras nor in Cochin. Within a couple of hours upon arrival in Cochin, we were already boarded on the boat. It was a huge Italian ship, full of tourists from New Zealand, Australia, and Sri Lanka. After the routine check of passport, visa and ticket, we were guided by a ship's employee to our sleeping compartments. We were settled in a big room with bunk beds and small personal space but quite comfortable. Remember that we were just trainees traveling at the cheapest fare, and the boat couldn't afford to offer us luxury at that price!

I still remember crystal clearly the sunset on the Arabian Sea when the boat whistled and slowly receded from the shoreline, departing just like the train in Calcutta. Another goodbye and a few more tear drops! The environment of the boat was quite joyful though, since most of the passengers from Australia and New Zealand were tourists going back to Europe on a long vacation to see their relatives after many years. There were many German families who were visiting their homeland after decades. They offered to give us free lessons in conversational German, and I realized later that it was the most useful language training with lots of fun that we ever had.

The next port was Eden, and the stop was short. Then the ship entered the Red Sea, traveling slowly up to the Suez Canal. We could see on the right-side Israel and Egypt on the left; and all the history and geography of these two countries we learned in our Mitra school flashed back. In those years the strongman of Egypt was President Gamal Abdul Nasser, a great friend of our first Prime Minister of free India: Jawaharlal Nehru. I remembered the trio of N: Nasser, Nehru, and Nkrumah!

Most of the workers on board were Italian, and they were very helpful knowing that we were young Indians leaving our country for a foreign land for the first time. Most of us were not used to European food habits. I didn't even know how to hold the cutlery set for eating properly at a table! Each table had two big jars of wine, one red and the other white; they were all included in our travel fare. Some of our friends enjoyed the drinks. I didn't try, not because I was a 'good boy' but simply because I was afraid of getting sick. I never touched alcohol in India, and my ignorance helped me to not get into the habit of drinking. In the evening after dinner, there was music and dance in a very lively environment. As you know, both Italians and Germans are great music lovers. I enjoyed the bands but didn't know how to dance. I simply felt good looking at others dancing at a cheerful pace with the music.

Many of the families that were on board were coming from New Zealand and Australia to Europe, mainly to Italy and Germany after several decades, essentially to tighten their old, ancestral family ties and spend a long vacation. So, the environment was full of joy. We, the Indian and Sri Lankan students and trainees, were treated by them as good and younger friends. They were always very helpful in every respect. The German families gave us free lessons on conversational German and gossiped with us in their native tongue!

After crossing the Suez Canal when the ship entered the Mediterranean Sea, rolling and pitching of the boat started due to the sea waves. This was something new to us and some of us became quite sick and vomited. Our German fellow travelers and friends took very good care of us during that time. Finally, we reached the first European port, Messina in Sicily. We could get out to give a walking tour of the port. It was so different from the Indian and Arabian ports in Cochin and Eden. It was a lively environment with soldiers and sailors giggling in the open air bars and restaurants on the sidewalks or walking gallantly with their usually "temporary" seaport girlfriends easily available at the port. We also had a long walk through the winding paths of the port along the seashore, through the pedestrian restaurants and bars, except that we couldn't have a drink at the bar, a nice dinner in an open-air restaurant, or a walking female companion at the port. All such amusements needed more money than we could afford.

The next port was Naples, and the stop was rather short. Many passengers, mainly the Italian tourists, left us here to meet their long waiting families and friends. The stopover was too short for us to get down and walk around the port. The final stop was in Genoa. Here we all left the boat that gave us merriment and refuge for twelve days with food and shelter. This was the departing moment to say *adieu* to our friends.

Some were going to England and the others in different parts of Switzerland and Germany. We got into a train that was transiting through the rest of Italy, then Switzerland and finally stopping in Stuttgart, Germany. There were two checkpoints, one at the entry of Switzerland and the other at the entrance of Germany. We didn't have to get off the train. The guards went into the train compartments and checked our passports and visas. They were very friendly with us and most of them spoke in English. We had no language problem!

As the train slowly entered the rail station of Stuttgart, it reminded me of the Howrah station of Kolkata. The floor of the platform was surprisingly camera-caught clean here, no comparison with our densely populated Howrah station! As the train stopped, I could see my friend Ranjit Sengupta, waving his hand and quickly approaching my compartment. First, we had a long, big, and strong hug. Then he helped me to get those small suitcases out of the train compartment. "How was the trip?" he asked eagerly. "Oh, fantastic! A great new experience! I never had a boat ride before. It was so exciting!" I replied. He must had noted my excitement on the face, and gave on my shoulder a friendly pat. We got out of the station after the usual check out and got onto a local public bus that took us almost right in front of Ranjit's residence. My luggage of two small suitcases was no problem to get out of the bus and then move up the stairs to the second floor of the house where he had a rented room with a shared kitchen with another resident, a student at the Technical University of Stuttgart. In those decades, the technical universities in Germany were termed "Technische Hochschule", translating that literally as "Technical High School ", sounds funny in English! (Professor Werner Heisenberg from the *"Technical High School"* of Munich received a Nobel Prize in Physics!).

I accompanied Ranjit to the kitchen, and he prepared for both of us a nice breakfast with toast, fried eggs with *sunny-side-up* and deliciously hot coffee. After breakfast we went out to walk around his neighborhood. Everything looked so spick-n-span clear as compared to my lifelong experience in Kolkata that I felt walking with Ranjit a long way without feeling any tiresomeness of my previous overnight train journey. Then we took a streetcar just like our tramways in Kolkata, and it traveled on a winding route all the way to the top of the mountain that surrounded Stuttgart. I still remember that area called Dagger-Loch. In that very fresh mountain air, we sat at an open-air café and relaxed with coffee and apple strudel while conversing on our good old years at Presidency and Jadavpur. Ranjit was eager to know about the whereabouts of our other friends at Jadavpur, and I gave him a good résumé of their status, both at work and pastime. We stayed for a long time at the café just enjoying the fresh air and the lovely scenery around. Ranjit gave me some ideas about the way of living a daily life in Germany including his own routine. We spent most of the afternoon in that hilly area viewing the wonderful sunset from the mountains. Then we took the same tramway down to Stuttgart where Ranjit lived.

For our evening meal we went to a nearby cafeteria rather than cooking at home. Again, I was amazed by the German cleanliness everywhere, from the streets to the buildings, in such a big city like Stuttgart. We came back after our dinner and slept early as Ranjit had plans to take me to Eningen/Reutlingen where I was supposed to start my training. He also wanted to introduce me to my new employer and thus the opportunity to get to know him personally.

Eningen was attached to Reutlingen, a city known for its textile institute and for its prosperity. People used to name it "Millionaires city". It was more of a big town rather than a city. Stuttgart was the only big city nearby, the capital of Württemberg province. The next smallest city of the province was Ulm (where Einstein was born!) and Tübingen, famous for its university specializing in Medicine and Arts.

The next morning, Ranjit and I left early after a good breakfast, again made by Ranjit, and took a public bus to Reutlingen. Public transportation in West Germany was excellent in those days. Only the rich had a Mercedes and the common people of the upper middle class had VWs, but most of the people preferred to take public transportation, which was cheaper and most importantly, very punctual. It took roughly an hour to reach Reutlingen, and then we took the tramway, *Streßenbahn* in German, to Eningen. It took only about fifteen minutes. Because of its smaller population in those years, Eningen was not even considered as a town; it was a village, *'Dorf'* in German. But a very picturesque one, as I came to experience later during my one year of living there.

We met the owner of the factory, Mr. Wilhelm Haarmann, in his house instead of in the plant. Ranjit arranged all these things in time by talking with Mr. Haarmann on the phone. His fluency in German, indeed, helped. We took a cab to reach his place. That was the first time we had taken a taxi since I arrived in Stuttgart. Here, the tips are fixed, twenty percent of the basic taxi fare. Later I came to know that it was the same percentage all over, even for the waitresses in restaurants and cafés. Germans love to standardize everything. That is why the German industrial standard, DIN (*Deutsche Industrie Norm*) is so popular in Central Europe!

Mr. Haarman received us at the gate of his bungalow. He was a tall and handsome pipe-smoking gentleman. As we entered with him and settled down in the living room, he introduced us to his wife, a slim and chic lady in her mid-thirties (I forgot her name!) and the two little kids, a boy of about 10 and a girl, roughly about a couple of years younger than the boy. Haarmann was in his late forties. Later I came to know that she was his second wife. The kids were very friendly, and Ranjit immediately started playing with them. Again, his command of German made him very friendly with the two kids in a few minutes! Together we spent a lovely afternoon. With my limited German I could still communicate with them.

Ranjit had to leave us to get back to Stuttgart. Before he left us, Mr. and Mrs. Haarmann took us to the second floor and showed us a small room neatly decorated with simple furniture, a single bed, a small table and a chair and the closet. Mr. Haarmann told me that I would be using that room till he could find a place for me near the factory. He added that I would go with him and come back with no transportation problems. Ranjit was elated at the hospitality of the owner of a factory to a simple trainee who just arrived! Before Ranjit left, we all sat together and had our dinner. In Germany, at least in those days, the lunch used to be a warm meal and the dinner was cold cuts, fruits and tea, coffee, beer, or wine for drink. There was a German saying: Breakfast like a Kaiser, lunch like a king and dinner like a Bertelsmann, meaning a poor man or beggar. But we had a good dinner with cheese, sausage, ham, and several fruits. As I realized later while living in Germany, that proverb was a bit exaggerated. We have a similar saying in Latin America: I won't share my breakfast with nobody; lunch I'd love to share with my best friend; and dinner, I'd give it to my worst enemy.

After Ranjit left, Mr. Haarman helped me to take my two suitcases up the stairs to my room, and with a smile, said softly, "Now you take rest. You must be tired from the journey. Tomorrow at 7 am meet us at breakfast. Gute Nacht!" I changed into my pajamas, read a bit of the very popular newspaper, *Bild Zeitung,* full of pictures from cover to cover, not much of the text, but it was good for me to learn German! Then I switched off the light and sank into the bed.

I was very careful about getting up and being on time at the breakfast table next morning, knowing a bit about German punctuality and discipline. Sharp at 7 am I went down and found Mr. and Mrs. Haarmann and the two kids already at the breakfast table waiting for me. German breakfast is very elaborate, including eggs, cheese, ham and sausages, lots of bread, a variety of fruits and coffee for the adults and hot chocolate for the kids. No wonder the Germans say: Breakfast is like a Kaiser.

I got the ride with Mr. Haarmann, the owner of the company! It took only a few minutes to reach the factory. Mr. Haarmann introduced me to a few colleagues and the head technician, Herr Meister. I'm recalling things from some sixty years ago, and don't remember his exact name; so I'll call him Herr Meister. Herr Meister gave me a light blue colored lab coat, the same kind he was wearing. No, I didn't have to "hold all" type factory worker's aprons, nor did I have to punch timecards. I was treated respectfully as an "Engineering Trainee", equivalent to EIT in the US, and not as a regular worker. But I had to work on the machines, like Capstan Lathe, Turret Lathe, Milling Machine, etc. like any other worker. That was a great practice which helped me a lot in the later years in my profession both in industries and in teaching. *"Übung macht den Meister!"* as the Germans say! I didn't want to be a "Theoretical" Engineer neither in industry nor in academia.

The factory was a small one. It produced small-sized tools and cutter grinding machines that we generally use for sharpening tools. The company had clients in other parts of Europe including Spain and Portugal, as well as in many developing countries of Africa and Asia. Later, when I got very friendly with Mr. Haarmann, I joked once, saying, "Maybe due to your clientele in India, you gave me a chance to be trained in your workshop, and then give me a job here." He simply smiled with an affectionate pat on my shoulder. Herr Meister, the Berliner, was also very friendly with me. He taught me with a lot of patience how to handle all the machines they had in the workshop. After six months of practice from hand-held tools to Capstan and Turret lathes, I was transferred to the Design Office. The office was small but cozy. There was only one draftsman, one secretary and one accountant. Thus, we had an excellent group for interacting during spare time. Mr. Haarmann would drop by from time to time to check on us.

The draftsman was an immigrant from East Germany, and he had a totally different German accent. Mr. Haarmann was also not a local person; he came from Rhineland and had a different but very clear accent. The rest of us (including myself with the team!) were locals with a heavy Swabian dialect. It is such a crooked German, not only just the accent but in many colloquial expressions, that even the Germans had problem in understanding them. Mr. Meister, even after living here for so many years, had sometimes trouble understanding the Swabian accent! I used to joke in my later years: I first learned "Schwabisch", then German!

The local people in that area are basically farmers, very simple and open-minded folks. After a week of staying with the Haarmanns, Mr. Haarmann found a family for me who had a house close to the factory and I stayed there as a paying guest. It was very convenient for me to walk only about ten minutes to reach my workplace. This family again had an interesting history. They were Germans who lived in Yugoslavia for many generations and recently moved back to Germany because of the political upheaval in Yugoslavia during President Tito's time. This was an elderly couple with three grown-up children. He still worked somewhere as a handyman, and she was a typical "Doctorate" house spouse taking care of everything of the family affairs from housecleaning to weekly shopping. Their eldest son, Hans, was about my age, and soon we became very good friends. The next was Fritz who was working somewhere as a fitter and the youngest was a daughter, Inge who was still going to a vocational school. I became so close to this host family that I started calling her *mammy*, and she started treating me as one of her kids, mainly Hans who was my age.

That was a time when many Indians came to West Germany for work or for training purposes. In a small place like Eningen, I met four Indians: Sachin, Thakur, Sudhir and Redey. Sachin and Thakur were from Bengal, Sudhir from Punjab, and Redey from Maharashtra. I could talk with Sachin and Thakur in our native tongue Bengali but with the others we spoke mainly in English. There was also a research scholar at the Textile Institute in Reutlingen. I have forgotten his name, but I remember that he was working for his Doctorate Degree at the institute. We Indians used to meet at the weekends, go to the bigger city of Reutlingen to eat and drink beer and have a good time together. Eventually, the neighborhood 'kids' of our age became friendly with our Indian group and started hanging around with us in the weekends. Thus, we ended up with a bigger group for lunching together and having fun in Reutlingen.

Then came the time of *"Fasching"*, a series of Folkfests in Southern Germany. They had many names: Ruthenfest, Schutzenfest, etc., each place having a different name for its festival. Sometimes we would walk in a group all the way to Reutlingen to take part in these fests, mainly eating hot sausages with bread, drinking beer and dancing in the open air with the local orchestra. This way we met new friends, both boys and girls of our age. I befriended a very interesting girl called Gerda. She was from Eningen but worked in Stuttgart, coming home during the weekends. I met her while looking for a partner to dance with. She taught me how to dance to the local music in proper steps!

One year of training in Wilhelm Haarmann KG went real fast. I learned the basic things in design for manufacturing small machines like a tool and cutter grinder as well as working on a Capstan lathe, Turret lathe, universal milling machine, etc. Working on a machine gave me the feelings of manufacturing that we learned before theoretically with not much practice. Socially, it was one of my best years. I met people from a different culture, stayed with their families and most importantly made good friends, both Indians and Germans who made me feel so good even when I'm writing these lines after some sixty years.

By the end of March 1973, the German Indian Association in Stuttgart arranged for me another apprenticeship of one more year. This time it was a much bigger manufacturing plant, Maschinenfabrik Weingarten, also in Württemberg province in a lovely area of Southern Germany, near the Lake of Constance *(Boden See)* and within a stone's throw from both Switzerland and Austria. It was a real tourist area, and we used to get a lot of tourists from Denmark, Sweden, and from other countries of Northern Europe. The company arranged a room for me in the home of a family near its factory. This time I was not lucky enough to stay with the factory owner's family for a whole week like I did upon my arrival from India.

My training was mainly in the design office. The company used to manufacture a variety of punch presses of industrial capacity, including multi-spindle transfer presses that produced the body parts of automobiles. My training was in the area of single-spindle presses, the simplest ones. The head of our department was Mr. Krausen, another Rhinelander like Mr. Haarmann. Most of the other colleagues were locals, except two co-workers, Mr. Rieger and Mr. Wünsche, who migrated from East Germany. The company also received many students as part-time employees in the design offices during their summer vacation, usually from late May till early September. Weingarten was really on an industrial belt, with Friedrichshafen, an industrial hub nearby and the engineering college in Konstanz was even closer.

Those days we didn't have computers, not even the mainframe ones. We had big drawing boards and we had to draw everything by hand with setsquares and T-square. The huge design hall for single-spindle press design was arranged in rows and columns of drawing boards, each with an accompanying working table. Each one of us had enough comfortable space to work and move around. The colleague on my right side was Mr. Schefhold, and to my left was Mr. Meyer; in front of me was a nice girl of about my age, Gisela Werker, and behind me was Mr. Rieger. We all enjoyed our company while working and during the coffee breaks. Lunch was provided free by the company in an industrial size cafeteria within its complex. It was only a few minutes' walk from our design office. We started work at 7 AM. Hence, breakfast was within the working hours. There were two secretaries who would come to each desk to take the breakfast order. It was usually a cold breakfast with bread, cheese, sliced ham, etc. plus a nice and hot coffee that was especially attractive during the cold months.

In those years, drinking beer at a workplace was allowed in Germany. It was just for quenching thirst, not for getting drunk. Beer was a socially acceptable drink in Germany at anytime, anywhere. There was even a popular saying in South Germany: Beer is for drinking and water is for washing. And it was true in daily life. Sweetened soda water was mainly for the kids. My daily breakfast and lunch were in the same factory and my dinner was very light in some nearby restaurant or cafeteria, or cold-cuts and fruits in my room. My room was on the ground floor right near the entrance. It was a small house, and my room was the only one on the ground floor adjacent to the stairs going up to the first floor. The house belonged to two elderly ladies, the two sisters in their seventies. I was surprised to observe how hardworking they were! They had a big vegetable and fruit garden, and they used to work all day there planting new vegetables, collecting the ripe ones for sale and for their own use as well as throwing the rotten ones in the rubbish, thus cleaning the entire plot every day!

Weingarten, like Eningen, was a small place but was very famous for its Basilica, an incredibly beautiful church with a huge dome of medieval architecture. The nearest bigger town or city was Ravensburg. Here also I met several Indian friends who worked in Ravensburg and in Biberach, another nearby smaller town. Both Ravensburg and Biberach had many manufacturing industries, both mechanical and chemical since they were both within the industrial hub of Southern Germany. Among my Indian friends, Kanan Ray and Nayan Ganguli lived and worked in some mechanical engineering plants in Ravensburg, and Tapas Goswami and Susthir Datta worked at a chemical factory in Biberach. On the weekends we used to get together in Ravensburg where Kanan and Nayan lived. The landlady was an elderly lady in her early seventies. She was extremely kind to all of us. We used to call her *mammy*.

Mammy would bring us a big jar of hot milk and bread for breakfast on the weekends before her regular visit to the nearby church. She used to refer to us as "My Indian Children" *(Meine Indische Kinder!)* when she had to introduce us to her visitors, mainly her relatives and friends. Mammy lived alone on the ground floor.

Social life in Ravensburg was a bit different from what I enjoyed in Eningen. In Eningen I lived with a Garman family. Their children, like Hans, and the neighborhood kids such as Erich and Heinz, were friends of mine and of Sachin, Sudhir, Thakur and Redey. We used to hang out together. It was really a German Indian Association in its true sense. Sometimes, I would come from Weingarten to Eningen for a long weekend to stay with them. In Ravensburg, we had no such intimate friendship with the local Germans, only neighborly acquaintances. Our only German caretaker was our *mammy*! It was a great feeling to have a mother far away from home.

On April 1, 1964, I completed one full year of training in Maschinenfabrik Weingarten AG and started thinking of my next 'Quantum Jump' in preparation for an engineering profession, while continuing working in the Design Office no. 1 (Technisches Büro 1). There were several alternatives.

I applied for Graduate Studies at the Technical University of Stuttgart. My professor at Jadavpur, Dr. Jaydev Das, did his Doctorate in Engineering (Dr. Ing.) under Professor Alfred Ehrhardt at Stuttgart. So, I wrote a letter to Professor Ehrhardt, giving reference to his ex-student Dr. Das and requesting an interview. He immediately replied very enthusiastically and then we talked on the phone to fix a date and time for the interview. His accent on the phone sounded very local: Swabian! He suggested a date and time to meet him in his office, and I agreed. Then I started preparing for the interview and the trip to Stuttgart.

On the day of interview, I took the same route that brought me from Reutlingen to Ravensburg a year ago! It was a lovely train journey along the winding way full of green valleys with a few small hills in between. I had a seat at the window to enjoy the beautiful scenery. It was soothing to the eyes and to my mind as well, since I was preparing mentally for a very important interview that could change my life to a totally different career. I kept pondering on the imminent interview with Professor Ehrhardt: What would he ask me? How should I answer him?

The train reached Stuttgart railway station on time. Memories flashed in my mind: The same station where Ranjit received me as I reached a foreign destination two years back. How time flies! The university was not too far from the railway station. I took a public bus that stopped right in front of the main campus gate. Then I walked about ten minutes to reach the Machine Tools Research Laboratory where Professor Ehrhardt had his office. He was also in charge of that research lab. I reached sharp at 10 AM, knocked at his door, and a mild voice responded: *Herein*. As I entered, I saw a small man with white shirt and black-framed glasses sitting in front of a huge executive desk and writing something in hand. No, there was no laptop in those decades. Professor got up quickly like a spring, walked around that huge table and shook my hand warmly. He was really of a very short structure, maybe five feet in height, slim but strong (with no typical German beer-belly!). Then he went back to his seat and asked me to sit down on the chair in front of him. I was still obviously a bit nervous, (despite his warm handshake!), thinking what he would possibly ask as a first inquiry. He noticed the nervousness on my face, smiled and told me to just relax for a few moments.

His first question was: How are you feeling in Weingarten? I replied that I was very satisfied with my job in the machine design office, and I had very good colleagues there who were always eager to help me. He seemed to be happy with my answer. Then I showed him my papers that I arranged very carefully in my briefcase: my bachelor's degree at Jadavpur and the work certificates from Remington in Calcutta and from Haarman in Eningen. He glanced over them and handed them back to me, nodding his small head in a positive gesture. I felt good. Then he asked me a few things about my design work in Weingarten, but the questions were not too technical. Then he embarked on inquiring joyfully about his ex-student Professor Jaydev Das at Jadavpur. He was also recollecting from his own memory when Dr. Das came to Stuttgart and became his research student many years ago. He was all the time smilingly remembering small anecdotes when Jaydev Das just joined his other research students and how they helped Jaydev, their fellow colleague, first to learn German (and of course, Swabian!). Professor Ehrhardt flattered me by commenting that my German was very good! He casually asked me where I learned such a good German; and I had to tell him the entire story of my language training.

In the third year at Jadavpur, I enrolled myself in a German language course offered by Herr Fischer, who worked full time at the West German Consulate in Calcutta and volunteered to give that course free at our university. During those years all European governments, namely, USA, Canada, Australia, Germany, Russia and even the UK wanted to offer a sincere helping hand to India, just emerging out of the darkness of almost two centuries of cultural colonialism. Mr. Fischer was a delightful person, always making all kinds of jokes regarding his own experience in learning Bengali and Hindi in India.

After two years of basic German with Mr. Fischer, when I graduated from Jadavpur and started working in Remington, I started taking some private lessons from Mrs. Grünstadt, an elderly Jewish lady who fled Germany during the Hitler years. Learning with Mrs. Grünstadt used to be very relaxing without any rigid timetable or books. I remembered my mother teaching me at home until grade 3! It was mainly practicing spoken Deutsch. Sometimes, she would just stand in the kitchen preparing her lunch or eating soup in her breakfast nook and talking fluently in German with me. I'd protest: Mam, I am not understanding anything! She would pat me on the shoulder affectionately and assure confidently: Don't worry! Just pay attention to the sound. Then she would continue with a teasing tone: And I'll pay my attention to your paying attention to my words!

When I told him all these events that happened way back in Calcutta, Professor Ehrhardt was impressed, and told me that he would take me as his Graduate student starting in September 1964. It sounded like something of a sensational news forecast to me when he uttered that sentence! I was so happy to hear his positive voice that I couldn't hide my emotion. I just got up from my chair in front of him and stretched my hand for a warm handshake showing my gratitude. If it were in India, I would have surely touched his feet!

I had a full copy of all my credentials in my briefcase. I handed them to him, and he asked me to follow him to the next door, his secretary's office. He handed them over to the secretary, a beautiful blond lady probably in her fifties. She quickly glanced over the papers and put them carefully in a metal file drawer. There were no paperless, computerized filing systems in those days. There were no laptops or smartphones like today. Professor Ehrhardt gave her a big smile from his small face, looked at me and assured me that I would get a letter of admission in a couple of weeks. In those days, especially at a European university, the procedures of admission in Graduate studies were short and simple; and a Full Professor had a lot of power in decision making. Professor Erhardt's words were enough for me.

After returning to Ravensburg I was fancying my Graduate Studies at Stuttgart; and the letter of admission really arrived in two weeks, as Professor Ehrhardt assured me. But I was also thinking of other alternatives. During the 1960s Canada was offering "Resident Visa" to professionals from other countries, especially from Europe and Asia, and the opportunities to immigrate to Canada because Canada was (and still is!) an under-populated country as compared to its neighbor, USA. Many Germans and our fellow Indians who were working in Germany, were getting Permanent Resident's Visa very quickly from the Canadian Consulates all over in Germany. I called the Canadian Consulate in

Stuttgart one day and asked for an interview after explaining my education in India and professional training in Germany in mechanical engineering. I also mentioned that unlike many Germans, I had no problem with the English language, especially technical English, since the four-year Bachelor of Mechanical Engineering degree curriculum and all its courses were offered in English in India. The lady on the other end of the phone line responded: Your English is very good, not at all a problem for us! Obviously not, as we were talking on the line in English, she in her Torontonian accent and I with my East Indian" *Banglish"* that the British taught us when they formed the East Indian Company in Calcutta before quickly colonizing the entirety of India.

We fixed a date for the interview, and I had to take the same train trip to Stuttgart to present myself at the Canadian Consulate. The interview was at 11AM, and I was on time. The gentleman who took my interview was a very young and handsome person. He had a really posh office, much nicer and bigger than that of Professor Ehrhardt. He was also a very polite gentleman, opening and holding the door for me to enter. At first, we had an easy chat. Then I handed the copies of my credentials to him, exactly the identical copies of the papers I gave to Professor Ehrhardt only a few weeks ago. He took time to look at them very carefully but didn't ask me any technical questions. Most probably he was not professionally a technical person but prepared with work experience in business administration or in sales. Anyway, he also assured me that I would get a letter in a couple of weeks. At the end he asked me a very important question. He asked with a nice assuring smile: When will you be able to travel to Canada to join us? I responded after a short pause: roughly around September. I thought before replying that if I would not start my studies again at Stuttgart, I should not waste my time in Germany. That way the month of September was a good target whether joining the Technical University at Stuttgart or leaving for Canada.

Eventually I decided to emigrate to Canada to start a new chapter in my life. I had to write a nice letter of apology to Professor Ehrhardt for not accepting his offer to start Graduate Studies under him. He answered with a very polite letter. This is the virtue of a good professor and a great human being! It was so inspiring that I tried to follow it throughout my own academic life in future. Another reason for choosing Canada was the English language. Although after working in Germany for over two years, my German was reasonably good for starting my studies again, but I preferred English to German for Graduate research.

The immigration visa came quite quickly from the Canadian Consulate, and I started winding up my net of connections in Germany and slowly unwinding with my friends. My Indian friends in Ravensburg and Biberach already started celebrating my departure, inviting me every now and then for dinner and drinks. Only *mammy,* our landlady felt sad for losing one of her "Indische Kinder". I also felt a bit of my pensive mood thinking that I would be missing her affectionate touch, her fingers crawling softly through my hair, her positive vibes whenever I had any problem. Besides, I'd miss that jug of warm milk she used to bring for us every Sunday morning for our breakfast. Also, I'd miss the great company of Nayan and Kanan every weekend evening for our adventures in the clubs and bars.

My office colleagues in Maschinenfabrik Weingarten also gave a farewell lunch party. It was not a fancy event but full of sincerity and most importantly, full of good feelings at my success in getting the opportunity to continue working in Canada. It was a very joyful lunch that I can remember crystal clear even today. Mr. Olsen, the Rhinelander, our boss, gave a short speech describing how nicely I mingled with the group and that my good command in German language helped in learning the design work quickly. My close colleagues like Meyers, Gut, and Gisela said that they would surely miss my company.

There were always a few things in preparing for a transatlantic trip for the first time: Buying the air ticket from the Lufthansa office in Ravensburg, closing the bank account and purchasing some traveler's cheques in US dollars. The factory also gave me some money as an end-of-service bonus! With that fund I bought a new suitcase, as the one brought from India was tearing apart from traveling too often between Ravensburg and Reutlingen. I also purchased a nice light blue colored three-piece suit, as the one from India was old fashioned. My friends from Biberach, Tapas and Susthir, came the next weekend and stayed two nights – Friday and Saturday – with us. In both the evenings we went out partying, and on Sunday afternoon they wished good luck to me in Canada and bid me farewell with goodbye hugs. I bought my air ticket to fly out during the weekday, on a Wednesday, as it was cheaper than on the weekend. Nayan and Kanan accompanied me to the train station in Ravensburg. It was an early morning train that would connect me to Stuttgart International Airport for a nonstop afternoon flight to New York. Again, after warm goodbye and *bon voyage* hugs from Kanan and Nayan I slowly got into the train compartment. I remembered my departure from the Howrah train station in Kolkata three years ago and from Reutlingen a year and a half back. Different places but the same feeling of nostalgia!

In New York, the World Fair of 1964 was going on in full swing! I took advantage of it by staying for a week at the YMCA in Slone House, right in downtown New York City. It was very inexpensive and safe accommodation, only $2.50 a night. The fairground was huge with exhibition tents from almost all countries of the world. The German pavilion was impressive with its colorful exhibition of the industrial products. I also visited the pavilions of India, Thailand, Japan, and many other Asian countries. The weather in NYC in September was still nice and warm. I walked around a lot throughout the exhibition halls and ate in open-air restaurants and food stands. This way I got the first taste of the typical American fast food: Burger, Fries and Sausages. One week really went fast in my delightful first experience on American soil, especially on the ground of the World Fair 1964 in NYC!

One evening while at Slone House YMCA, I called my Professor, Dr. Ram Mukherjee of Jadavpur University, who was at that time enjoying a year of Sabbatical Leave at Rutgers State University in New Jersey. Professor Mukherjee was very happily surprised to receive my phone call from New York, and immediately invited me to spend a few days with him at his residence in New Jersey. I agreed delightfully, checked out from the Slone House YMCA the very next day, and took a bus to New Jersey. I called him before leaving the New York bus station. As I arrived at the New Jersey bus terminal, he was already waiting there! It was a great feeling for me to meet him again in a totally different environment. He gave me a big hug and then took me to his apartment within the university campus. He was living alone and had a car to drive me around the university campus and the city of New Jersey.

The next day he showed me his lab and introduced me to some of his colleagues and Graduate students. However, to me it was more exciting to move around the city and to eat in different places outside and get a taste of a new continent that I had landed on only a week back. Everything was so different from India and Germany! Here you hardly find a big mass of people walking along the sidewalk. Everyone seemed to have a car of some sort. The restaurants and food-stands were different, and unlike in Germany, you couldn't drink beer everywhere!

Three days with Professor Ram Mukherjee passed very quickly. I remember, he advised me, "Your almost three years of industrial experience was great. Now is the time for Graduate studies!" His wife and his two brothers were still doing their Graduate studies in Tübingen, Germany at that time. Maybe that was the reason why he emphasized to me the importance of Graduate studies. Professor Mukherjee took me to the local city airport of New Jersey for a straight and short flight to Toronto, Canada. I touched his feet at the airport for blessing (this is an Indian custom of showing respect to the elders) and he touched my head with his right hand as a sign of blessings.

The flight was about an hour. Toronto airport looked so vacant compared to JFK in New York! I got the first sign of a sub-populated country, as I was told in Germany. The immigration procedure was fast, and an elderly officer stamped my passport with a "Landed Immigrant" status and with a broad, inviting smile on his face, said "Welcome to Canada!". I liked his friendly welcome. It was around 12 noon, and the day was bright. So, rather than staying overnight in Toronto, I took a bus to Kitchener where I was supposed to get a job as indicated by the Canadian Consulate in Stuttgart.

Kitchener was some sixty miles from Toronto Airport, and it took about an hour and half to reach there. Right across the bus terminus I saw the big sign of a hotel: Wolper Hotel. I walked slowly across the road with my two small suitcases and checked in. The lady at the reception noted the details of my immigration status from my passport, threw me a nice smile, and handed over the key for a room on the first floor. "Thank you so much!" I replied and took the stairs to the first floor carrying my two small suitcases.

The room was small but neatly furnished with a single bed, a desk, a chair, and a closet. Good enough for me. After putting the suitcases in the closet, I went out to eat something since I only had a light breakfast at Dr. Mukherjee's place very early in the morning. We were in a hurry to catch the flight for Toronto. I saw a small restaurant across the road and entered. The waitress came and I ordered a regular meal of baked Salmon, white rice, and salad. Again, I remembered, no beer in unlicensed restaurants in America! So, I asked for a Coke with no ice in it. The girl gave me a look of surprise, since in the USA and Canada, they fill the glass of a soft drink, first full of ice and then the liquid. After eating I went back to my hotel room, saw a bit of Canadian TV programming, and went to bed early. I was a bit tired from traveling.

The next morning, I went to the Employment Office, and to my good surprise I found my name already there as a Landed Immigrant. I was very impressed! The Employment Officer, again a young gentleman like the one at the Canadian Consulate in Stuttgart, held the interview. He gave me a forwarding letter, stating that I am a mechanical engineer with three years of practical experience in West Germany. He advised me to take the letter to the factory named Jerry Hydraulics for a position.

The next morning, I went straight to Jerry Hydraulics without making any previous phone appointment. It was a small manufacturing factory making parts for hydraulic pumps and other related equipment. Mr. Morgen, the manager, a tall and large guy, received me in his office, and asked me about my experience in Germany. Once I showed him all my credentials, he gave me a position in the Quality Control department and introduced me to the head of that department. Mr. Morgen was originally from Austria and here his position was the head of the Quality Control department; Mr. Walker was from Jamaica. The three of us got together in the factory's cafeteria, after our official interview was over, and we had a nice friendly chat. Mr. Morgen asked me where I was living. I said: Wolper Hotel, for the time being. He reacted: Oh, that is too expensive! "My in-laws have a house nearby, and they rent rooms to single workers. Would you like to see?". "Sure. That will be great!".

At lunchtime Mr. Morgen took me in his car to his in-law's home. It was only about a ten minutes' drive. An elderly lady, perhaps in her late sixties or early seventies, opened the door, and they kissed on the cheeks in the usual European way and greeted in German with a typical Austrian accent that I learned in Weingarten, not too far from Austrian border. There were many Austrians working in Southern Germany during the early sixties. Mr. Morgan introduced me to his mother-in-law in German, and the lady was a bit surprised to see a dark-skinned guy like me understanding and speaking in German. She gave me a warm handshake with a smile. She led both of us into the house and showed me a small vacant room neatly furnished with a single bed, a desk and a chair plus the closet, just like in the Wolper Hotel where I was staying. I agreed right away to be a rented guest. Mr. Morgan later in the afternoon helped me to get my luggage from the hotel. I checked out of the hotel and checked into my new residence. Everything got resolved quickly that afternoon.

The in-laws of Mr. Morgan were a great couple. All their children were grown up; they got married and moved out of their paternal home. So, they had three vacant rooms and the two of them were rented to single fellows like me. One was rented to Heinz, originally from Switzerland and the other to Tony, an immigrant from Holland. They were both about my age, and eventually we became good friends. We used to hang around a lot on the weekends, going out to the local bars for a few drinks and then to some moderate restaurants for a good but not too expensive dinner. This way we made other friends, both males and females, more or less of our age, while drinking and eating at the bars and restaurants over the weekends. There was also a night club right beside the factory of Jerry Hydraulics. It was named Schwaben Club. They had a nice ballroom dance orchestra every Saturday evening. Sometimes we three would go there to meet new people and to have a good time while dancing and drinking!

My work in Jerry hydraulics was making the dimensional measurements of the small products, checking their tolerance limits with "go and no go" gauges and drawing the Quality Control charts. It was an easy job that I learned at Jadavpur as a student. It was not the work of an engineer-in-training (EIT), rather it was the work of a technician. But I didn't care about any work status. I was only interested in working to save some money. My main aim for coming to Canada was to start my Graduate Studies as soon as possible. Mr. Walker, my Quality Control boss and I became good friends and both of us used to enjoy our two coffee breaks together in the factory's small cafeteria; he was remembering his youth in Jamaica, and I was telling him my stories in Germany. He used to ask me a lot of questions regarding my work environment in Germany.

While working in Jerry Hydraulics, I started inquiring about the possibilities of starting my studies at the University of Waterloo, a relatively new university, founded only about twenty years ago. It was established as an alternative to the University of Toronto, which was the biggest in the province of Ontario, and was extremely competitive to enter as a student, both in Undergraduate and Graduate schools. Also, Kitchener-Waterloo was a twin city, like Minneapolis-St. Paul in Minnesota or Urbana-Champaign in Illinois in the US universities. Besides, Kitchener-Waterloo was only sixty miles from Toronto. Waterloo was a good option vis-a-vis Toronto.

One morning I saw an ad in a local newspaper, looking for an "Intermediate Designer" in Sunshine Office Equipment, a firm in Waterloo that used to manufacture office furniture mainly from sheet-metals. I got curious for two reasons. It was the job of a designer, not just measuring nuts and bolts in a Quality Control room. Second, the factory was in Waterloo where the university was located! The next Monday, I took the phone and called. The voice that responded had a heavy British accent:" Hello, I'm Alex Wakefield. How can I help you?" I explained to him that I was responding to the newspaper ad looking for an office furniture designer. Then I told him about my Bachelor of Mechanical Engineering degree in India and three years of work experience in Germany. He got interested and we set a date and time for an interview. If I remember vaguely, it was set for next Wednesday at 9 AM! I had to take leave from my Jerry Hydraulics job for that day only. I talked with Mr. Walker, and he assigned me a day off right away without asking any questions. I was glad that I didn't have to tell him any details.

Early in the morning that Wednesday, I made a light breakfast at home, got ready and took the trolley that connected Kitchener with Waterloo. The factory was on Erb Street, only a few blocks from the trolley stop. From outside, the factory looked a bit bigger than Jerry Hydraulics. As I entered through the main gate and presented myself to the receptionist, she gave me a 'good morning' smile and took me to Mr. Wakefield's office. As she lightly knocked the door, a British accent responded: Come in, please. We entered and a thin figure got up from his desk, scattered with all kinds of papers. As I presented myself, we shook hands, "Hello, Jay, I am waiting to meet you!" and smiled with a face full of enthusiasm. All of a sudden, his gesture reminded me like a flashback to George Bernard Shaw's *My Fair Lady* when Professor Higgins met his colleague from India!

Mr. Wakefield and I had a very relaxed talk, and again I handed over to him a set of the copies of my credentials, the university degree, and the certificates of work experience in Germany. I made several such sets knowing that I'd surely need them for job hunting in Canada. Mr. Wakefield was very frank with me. He said that honestly the position that they advertised was not for a full-fledged mechanical engineer like me but for an intermediate designer of some moderate experience. When I further explained to him the kind of parts design work I did in Weingarten, he was convinced and offered me the position. When he asked when I could join, I responded eagerly: Next week. I could see in his eyes that he liked my positive attitude; and I liked his response: That is great, Jay!

Next morning, I had to inform Mr. Morgan and Mr. Walker that I would be leaving them soon as I got a better offer as a designer in Sunshine Office Equipment in Waterloo.

I was totally frank with both since they were equally frank and honest with me when they offered me the opportunity to work with them in Jerry Hydraulics. Mr. Walker was a bit disappointed since we were working together very well and at the same time developing a nice camaraderie. Unfortunately, or fortunately, life is a moving feast. I had to give the same news, good or bad, to the in-laws of Mr. Morgan and to Heinz and Tony. They were all very disappointed that I would be leaving them. And me too, since I used to hang around a lot with Heinz and Tony on weekend evenings. I would surely miss them.

The next step was to find a place to live within walking distance from Sunshine Office Equipment, my next hop to work. Again, I was lucky to find a young family, a university student, his working wife and two little girls. They lived in a small, rented house, next to my new workplace, and they had an extra room upstairs on the second floor. A student needs money and I needed a place to live. Thus, it was a good win-win deal, and on a fine weekend morning I moved to Waterloo. Another nostalgic farewell hug with Heinz and Tony!

My new landlord and landlady were a very young couple. He was a Physics student at Waterloo, and she used to work somewhere, sending her daughters to a daycare center nearby. I have forgotten their names; the little girls were Liza and Lorna. Every Sunday we used to have brunch together, and that was the time once a week we could talk a lot with no time limits. I was always invited by them; very generous indeed! The little girls used to get bored after a while, sitting silently on their highchairs. We used to put them down on the floor to play with their toys. There were no computer games in 1964, thank goodness!

I used to get a lot of information about Waterloo University from him. He was finishing his undergraduate degree in Physics, and looking ahead for Graduate Studies in Europe, hopefully in England. And I was around the same time coming from Europe for Graduate studies in Canada. So, we had a lot of ideas to share. He suggested that I should go to the university campus on a working day and inquire personally for admission in the Graduate school. Following his advice, I took leave for a day from my work and went to the Waterloo campus. It was within walking distance from my residence, crossing a large field all covered with snow in early December. Kitchener-Waterloo falls on a 'snow belt' and snowfall starts very early, sometimes even in September! Yes, I bought some light snow boots upon my arrival in Waterloo.

Upon reaching the university campus on foot one fine morning, cold but bright with sunshine, I headed straight to the Faculty of Engineering building. Mechanical Engineering offices were on the second floor. I saw the sign "Administrative Assistant" on one of the doors and entered. A very elegant lady in her late forties or early fifties was sitting in front of a small desk. As I wished good morning to her, she looked at me with a nice smile and responded amiably: Yes, what can I do for you? While I was explaining briefly my purpose of coming to get information on Grad studies in Mechanical Engineering, she was looking at me curiously and at the same time taking notes on what I was saying. I found this practice very efficient, doing two things at the same time! Remember, there was no Laptop in 1964.

After listening curiously to my short "talk", she got up, took a file in her hand and asked me to follow her. After passing by a few offices along the corridor, she stopped in front of one. I noticed on the door a nameplate: Prof. M. J.

Hillier. She knocked at the door gently, and again came a voice with a British accent: Come in, please. As we entered, I was quite nervous. She noticed it and quickly winked at me, assuring good, positive vibes. The professor, sitting in front of a huge desk, filled with books and papers all around, asked us to sit on the two chairs in front of him, and then looked up for the first time to see who we were. "Hello, Betty, good morning!" and then he said hi to me with a nod. Betty explained to him briefly why I was there with her. Then she left.

I was left alone in front of a professor! The last time I was in front of a big professor was at Stuttgart in Professor Ehrhardt's office. This was the second time again to be interviewed by another professor from Europe! I felt lonely. Professor Hillier felt my inner loneliness and asked with an assuring look: How are things coming up with you? (As if he knew me and my whereabouts!). This friendly approach gave me a good jolt, and very spontaneously I started talking about my plans. I had done this short speech many a time in my life, starting with Mr. Chitta Ghose in Remington Rand in Kolkata, Herr Haarmann in Eningen, Professor Ehrhardt at Stuttgart, and coming to Canada with Mr. Morgan in Jerry Hydraulics in Kitchener and Mr. Wakefield in Sunshine Office Equipment in Waterloo. I was by now an expert in telling my story!

After hearing my brief account, Professor Hillier started saying his part of what he could offer. He explained that he was building a manufacturing laboratory where some machines would be arriving next year, 1965. Some of these machines were supposed to come from Germany, he added, knowing that I worked over two years in machine tools manufacturing firms in Germany. His main area of research was the application of the mechanics of materials in manufacturing processes. He advised me to start on a specific problem, applying Plasticity in Forming Processes. I might have to build some small experimental testing set-up, and there were technicians in the department available to me to construct the experimental rig. The way Professor Hillier was talking was as if I was already accepted for admission in Grad studies to work under his supervision. And I was right!

After finishing his "talk", he got up from his chair. I noticed a middle-height man of about 5 ft 8 inches with a little beer belly. He asked me to follow him, and we ended up again in Betty's office. Betty helped me to fill in a few short forms while Professor Hillier went back to his office. He told me softly, "See me in my office after you are through with Betty" and left. Within ten minutes, I finished filling in all the admission forms and thanked her sincerely for helping me. She winked again, as if she had known me for quite a while, and wished me with a smile: good luck with Marc! I went back to Hillier's office. He gave me a few more instructions on manufacturing research and suggested that I should be getting a formal letter of admission soon and that I should be able to start sometime in January 1965. I was overjoyed when he uttered that last phrase! It was very similar to what I felt in Professor Ehrhardt's office in Stuttgart six months ago. Professor Hillier added that he would offer me a Research Assistantship (RA), two hundred Canadian Dollars a month; and the rest could be arranged from a Teaching Assistantship (TA) once I join the department. Two hundred Dollars per month was a good fund in those years for the survival of a single person like me with no other financial responsibilities, such as maintaining a family with little kids like my student landlord in Waterloo.

I felt really very lucky since I finished my undergrad studies at Jadavpur in May 1961. All these three and a half years of work experience as an Engineer-in-training (EIT) went past without any hassle in India, West Germany, and Canada. Now, this back-to-school-again feeling was hilarious! Next day I went to work as usual and broke the news to Mr. Wakefield. He replied, "Jay, I knew this would happen. You are too over-qualified for the job you are doing here. I wish you the very best in your Grad studies and research!" Then I told my colleagues that I would be leaving to continue my studies in January.

This was just before Christmas. Our Design Department had a Christmas Party. Mr. Wakefield combined my farewell celebration with the Christmas Party. We did it on the weekend just before Christmas Eve. We, the entire Design Department, spent a full day including a fabulous lunch and the traditional afternoon "High Tea" with lots of Canadian Beer: Black Label! That was a wonderful day full of Christmas spirit and the joy of the season plus my farewell party focused on it. I can never forget that day at the onset of going back to school again!

3
GRADUATE STUDIES AT WATERLOO

Once I received the official letter of admission by mail, I went to the Mechanical Engineering Department, and Betty fixed me a study desk in the Manufacturing Lab. The only other person in the lab was the technician, Bill Duench. I was glad to have an isolated place in a lab rather than in the Grad Students' Hall with so many students. Soon Bill and I became good friends sharing experience, my factory work in Germany and Bill's experience in Canadian industries before joining Waterloo. Just like with Mr. Walker in Jerry Hydraulics, Bill and I used to have our coffee breaks together. Bill was a machinist and worked on all types of machine tools: lathe, radial drill, universal milling machine, surface grinder, etc. Computerized Numerical Control (CNC) machines were yet to come in 1965!

Next to our Manufacturing Lab there was a small Metrology Lab with several measuring instruments and table-top optical microscopes. Another nearby lab was for the undergraduate students, mainly a teaching lab for demonstrating vibration, four-bar mechanisms, planimeters and all sorts of strain-gage type electrical measuring equipment. The supervisor of that lab was Professor Pierce, an elderly person in his late fifties or early sixties. Professor Pierce was looking for a "Demonstrator" in his lab. The demonstrator's job was to conduct the experiments for and with the students so that they get some hands-on experience. It is equivalent to Teaching Assistant (TA) in American universities. I was lucky to get that position. Probably because of my industrial experience in Germany, Professor Pierce selected me. It was an easy job, only once a week, but it gave me some extra money per month apart from the Research Assistantship (RA) that Hillier offered. Summing up TA and RA, it was a good income for a single student like me. I had no other financial responsibilities except maintaining my own expenses.

Gradually, I met other Graduate students of Hillier. He had several foreign students: Wahed Ali Mir from West Pakistan, Govind Lal and Gurnam Singh from India plus Pablo Barreto from Colombia, South America. Besides, he had several Canadian students and a few post-docs. He was a busy man in research but also offered one or two Graduate courses per year. He was a shy, single soul living in an apartment but spending most of the time in his office, writing research proposals and papers. There was a time in the pinnacle of his research career when he was publishing papers in refereed journals, almost one research article a month! He liked the American journals but used to publish mostly in British journals, maybe because of the academic connections he maintained with his colleagues in Imperial College at the University of London, including Professor Bill Johnson at UMIST in Manchester and his buddies at the University of Birmingham. Also, his research supervisor at Imperial College, a big guy, Professor J. M. Alexander, author of several standard Graduate level textbooks on Manufacturing Processes and Systems! All these "connections" also helped him publish his research results quickly in the leading journals in a most prolific way. Indeed, I was very lucky to work under him and have him as a guide and a mentor even after I left Waterloo with a Ph.D.

Gurnam, Pablo, and I used to hang out together a lot after our study hours. Govind used to join us from time to time. Mr. Mir was a very serious religious person. He used to pray five times a day, spreading a prayer mat beside his study desk; and absolutely no alcoholic drink! But he was a very nice person, a perfect gentleman. In those days, I didn't know any Spanish and Pablo used to tease me: Jay, when are you going to learn a bit of Spanish? I was quick in responding: And how about you, my dear friend, learning some Bengali? I was so ignorant about Latin America that I didn't know that Spanish was the third most widely spoken in the world, after Mandarin and English. Now, in 2022, it is the second most widely spoken language, after Mandarin and before English. This is because many Amerindian tribes in Latin America don't read or write Spanish, but they do speak!

Within a year after I joined, a professor from Australia brought his graduate student with him. Dr. Ralph Scrutton was the professor, and his student was Jim Thé, a Chinese-Indonesian Australian. Thus, we had the perfect international gang of graduate students in our manufacturing research, all the way from Australia to Latin America! Then Mr. Vedi came from India as Hillier's student. But he was a very serious type of person, like Mr. Mir. He was also a very religious Sikh. He was the only family man in our group. He came from India with his wife and two little kids. With Mr. Vedi and Mr. Mir, we were just good colleagues. Eventually, Pablo, Gurnam, Jim and I became good "buddies". We used to go out for a drink after a day's work in our labs. Later we joined a "Little Theater" group of artists who used to get together in a pub in downtown Waterloo. The pub was called Circus Room, a bit far from our campus, especially for walking in winter. So, I bought an old car: a 1954 Pontiac for 200 Dollars! The car was good enough for our transportation within Kitchener-Waterloo twin city, especially to go to our hang-out places on the weekends.

Next semester, in September 1965, two other Graduate students joined our Civil Engineering Department: Ildefonso Villareal from Monterrey, Mexico, and Imam Hossain from Comilla, East Pakistan (now Bangladesh). These two international students (we don't use the word "Foreign Student" anymore!) eventually entered our circle of good friends. Imam and I spoke Bengali as our native tongue. I was very glad to speak my own language again! Since I left my friends Nayan and Kanan in Ravensburg, almost a year ago, I didn't have a chance to speak in Bengali. Imam and I became close friends very quickly, maybe because of our common language, food habits, in sum our common Bengali culture.

In the manufacturing laboratory, Bill and I worked together. He had his desk right in front of mine and we used to spend a lot of time talking, sharing our ideas, as well as gossiping. For my Master's thesis I had to do some experimental work on bursting small and thin-walled cylinders under internal hydraulic (oil) pressure. Bill helped me to fabricate the experimental set-up. Professor Hillier used to smoke Cuban cigars ("Puros") and I used the aluminum tubes, the containers of the cigars, as my "thin cylinder" workpieces for the experiments. Those cigar-covers were ideal for my tests; they were only about five to six inches long, really thin-walled and an internal diameter of about three-fourth of an inch, just right for my experiments. The wall thickness was less than one-sixteenth of an inch, thus making it perfectly within the range of a "thin cylinder" for the cigar casings. Hilliar's smoking Cuban "puros" was quite a coincidence for my experiments! I still carry some of the photographs of those tests I conducted in our Manufacturing Lab at Waterloo in 1965.

My Master's thesis work also included some numerical results to compare them with the experimental outcome. Imam used to help me with numerical computation. The new IBM 360 mainframe computer had just arrived in the math department, covering almost the entire basement of the building. We had to punch a deck of cards for inputting the numbers and leave them overnight on the computer to get results the next morning for "debugging"! Today you can do those calculations on your personal laptop and get the results in a few minutes. Imam was very good at computing and gave me a good hand in writing my thesis quickly and then we'd go for a drink in the evening at Circus Room with the Little Theater group of artists. Imam himself was a talented artist. He was a magician and each time we had an art festival on campus, he was the performing magician. He was also a good fine arts nerd, making all kinds of humorous black-and-white sketches to entertain us. Another talented artist in our gang was Jim Thé. He was a good painter in color and exhibited his work in our yearly exhibition at Waterloo.

Around June 1966 I finished my work and started writing up the thesis. There were two other professors, apart from Hillier, to examine my thesis. One was Professor Archie Sherbourne, the Dean of Engineering, and the other was

Dr. Allan Plumtree, a new, young faculty member, also from England, who used to hang around a lot with the graduate students; Allan was really a jolly good fellow.

Incidentally, both the examiners were British. Maybe Hillier intentionally selected them, his fellow countrymen, to prevent any last-minute problem. Anyway, they both gave "green light" to my work and I got my Master of Applied Sciences (MASc) Degree in the October 1966 Convocation at Waterloo!

In the meantime, Pablo Barreto, my buddy, got married with a Colombian woman he met only a few months back in the hospital in Kitchener. She was a trainee nurse there. Her name was Dora. We had a big wedding party in the living room of a small two-bedroom apartment. Only our good gang of about eight to ten people and, of course, our boss Hillier were invited. It was a great party with good music and food and drinks. We got some local caterers to supply food and the drinks we brought. I remember Hillier smoking his peace pipe and enjoying it with us like a fellow graduate student. At midnight, Pablo and Dora left us in the VW bug that Pablo bought a few months ago. They reserved a hotel somewhere in a nearby resort, probably in Almira – a Mennonite village – for their honeymoon! But our party continued till almost when the daylight started tickling through the windows.

Pablo quickly finished his MSc as he had an offer from a General Electric (GE) Co. branch in Barrie in Northern Ontario, a couple of hours' drive from Waterloo. I remember Dora coming every now and then to our lab to "help" Pablo do his research experiments on Thin Plate Rolling! Soon he defended his thesis and the happy couple moved to Barrie. Gurnam and I went several times in my old 1954 Pontiac to check how they were doing. The car was very old but the memories it carried are still very fresh and alive. In January 1967, a huge Bohm Surface Grinder arrived from Hamburg, Germany to our manufacturing lab. As Hillier told me in the very beginning, almost two years previously, he put me to work on that machine, perhaps because of my work experience in Maschinenfabrik Weingarten. Bill and I worked together to level the foundation of the big machine and install it. Thus, our workplace had now two machines: a universal milling machine at one end of the hall and the surface grinder at the other extreme. We had a lot of space to move around. Professor Ralph Scrutton got another student, Mr. Kwan Luc from Hong Kong, and put him to work on the milling machine, and I started handling with that enormous surface grinder, first to understand it and then to work on it for my PhD dissertation.

One day Jim and I got an invitation from Toronto through his artistic connection. It was the birthday celebration of one of his fine arts groups in Toronto. We went, as usual, in my old Pontiac. The party was very lively, again in a big apartment like Pablo's wedding party, and there I befriended a woman l called Dedeng. She was from the Philippines and was working at a hospital in Toronto. Today she is back in her country after retirement, and we are still in touch. Every year I send her a birthday gift card to celebrate on February 1st! From Toronto she moved to Los Angeles in California and worked there for many years before retirement. Now she owns a hotel in Kalibo, in the Philippines, and her niece takes care of it.

Both Gurnam and I got busy with our experimental work. Mr. Mir also had to do some experimental studies on Deep Drawing. Pablo's set-up on Strip Rolling was taken by someone else. Professor Scrutton got another Indian student named Vijay Shankla. Thus, our manufacturing group under

Hillier and Scrutton got busy. We built good camaraderie amongst us, the Graduate students in manufacturing processes. Meanwhile we made two trips to Detroit with Hillier in his car. Hillier and Gurnam in the front seats, Mr. Mir and myself in the back seats. Gurnam was a good talker to keep us all well entertained during our two-hour trip. The main reason for the trip was to see some equipment and Detroit was the nearest big industrial hub. On both ways, back and forth between Waterloo and Detroit, we stopped a few times for lunch and coffee breaks. Hillier paid for all of us. He was always a very good hospitable host for his graduate students. He was also a single soul with a lot of money!

By March 1969, I finished my dissertation work and Hillier asked me to wrap up and start writing. I found a hiding place in a small building not too far from our engineering faculty and kept working there to finish up quickly in writing the first draft. No, I didn't show my buddies my escape hatch! I wrote in cursive rather than using an old typewriter. There was no Laptop in 1969! I used to finish a chapter and send it to Professor Hillier. He would correct it with red ink and return it to me. Just the old-fashioned editing without any machine except a ballpoint pen, but it worked well. Then I handed over the entire manuscript to Ricky, our new secretary who recently joined Betty's group a few months ago. Ricky came from Germany. With her German efficiency and promptness, she did the typing of my dissertation very quickly and almost with no error.

In June I had the oral defense of my dissertation. Professor Milton Shaw of MIT came as the external. Shaw was so famous that in one sense I was very happy to have him as my examiner and have his name signed in my work! But at the same time, I was quite nervous to face such a giant in manufacturing. The other external examiner was Professor Jim Church. He was in our Mechanical Engineering Department before (and I worked in the beginning as his TA) but he recently moved to a nearby technical college, Conestoga College of Science and Technology as the President. It looked to me like Professor Hillier selected the externals carefully so that I didn't get flunked in the final stage.

One evening Marc Hillier invited me for a few drinks in a local pub. We had some munchies and a few beers. During our conversation, he said that I had worked on a particular problem for my dissertation for almost three years, both the theoretical and the experimental parts of the research topic. Hence, none of the examiners including himself knew better than me. His idea of inviting me over for a few drinks, now I realize after so many years, was to get me out of my nervousness and fear. Even today I remember those lines and tell them to my own students before their exams. No, I don't invite them for drinks before their exams, understanding a different cultural background here in Latin America.

It was in the morning hours, I think at 10 AM, my oral exam was set. My buddies, Gurnam and Jim came with me to the lobby and assured me that they would be waiting in the aisle outside the room where the oral exam – viva *voce* in Latin - was supposed to take place. There were four guys in the room: Professors Shaw, Church, Hillier, and Scrutton, as I entered. I was introduced to Professor Shaw by my boss, Hillier. Professor Shaw stood up from his seat and shook hands with me. A tall and slim figure with a slightly balding head, and with a nice smile. As usual practice, I was given half an hour to present my work. I had that experience from last year's Applied Mechanics Conference in Minneapolis where I accompanied Professor Hillier and presented our paper. I was not nervous! Then the questions started. Professor Hillier, my supervisor was conducting the exam. He asked first Professor Shaw to ask the questions, then Professor Church, the second external and then Professor Scrutton as the Internal examiner, and finally Professor Hiller himself as the supervisor. That was the order of shooting!

Most of the questions from all the four examiners were of technical type. I answered them satisfactorily. It took about another half an hour to forty-five minutes to wrap up the question- answer session. Then Hillier asked me to go out of the room and wait in the aisle. As I got out of the room, there I found Gurnam and Jim waiting for me. "How did it go? "Jim asked. "I hope I made it. At least, I answered all their questions." I replied, now a bit nervously, for I was not sure what those four were going to decide. In ten minutes, the door of the room opened wide, and it was first Professor Shaw who came towards me with a smile, extending his hand for a handshake: "Congratulations, *Dr. Banerjee!*" I was elated to hear the word Doctor before my name, for the first time! Then the others congratulated me one by one. Professor Church winked at me with a smile.

It was almost lunchtime. Hillier invited all of us, even Gurnam and Jim, to have lunch in our Faculty Cafeteria where only the professors were allowed. It was the first time the three of us, still the graduate students, entered the faculty dining room! Later, I joked with Jim and Gurnam: See, you guys could get in because of me! During lunch, the professors talked about various things. Professor Hillier was going on Sabbatical Leave to Grenoble, France for a year. He explained to us about his plan. Professor Shaw asked me, "What are your plans now?" I told him that I had till December to decide and that I would write some papers for publication.

He suggested to me a few refereed journals where he was one of the technical editors. I felt very grateful for what he offered. Professor Church, the new President of Conestoga College, was very happy. He started talking about his current position that was for the first time a very responsible administrative position for him. He added, "Well, I'm still in the process of learning!"

After my defense was over, Professor Hillier started packing up for his Sabbatical in France. He asked me to start writing the papers for publication and suggested some refereed journals where he had already published many papers, and hence the chance of acceptance is high and fast. Before he left, we had a great open-air party around a swimming pool. It was a lovely day in summer. We spent the entire day till late afternoon, swimming, eating, drinking, and talking. A wonderful day to remember! This time, we - his students - collected money amongst us, and didn't let Hiller pay for the expenses of the party.

While working as a Postdoc from June till December 1969, I was also looking for a job. Among several applications, I got a good and positive reply from Douglas Aircraft (which is now Boeing Co.) in California. It was the position of a junior research engineer in their assembly section and the salary offered was very good. Simultaneously, I was looking for an opportunity for some international experience in South America through Canadian University Services Overseas (CUSO) with its headquarters in Ottawa. I applied there and had an interview in Ottawa. During the interview they mentioned that my positive point was that I lived cross-culturally in India, Germany and Canada, and the only negative point was that I knew no Spanish or Portuguese needed to work in Latin America. I gave an argument that since I already knew several languages, including Bengali, Hindi, Sanskrit, English, German and some beginner's French, it won't be very difficult for me to learn another language: Spanish or Portuguese.

I convinced the interview board with my argument, and they asked if I'd like to take a three-month intensive course in Spanish in Mexico. It would be an in-residence course in Cuernavaca, Mexico, from January till end of March 1970; and all expenses including airfare, room and board would be covered by CUSO. I immediately agreed!

Then they gave me some idea about the type of job I would be expecting. The University of Del Valle (*Universidad Del Valle*) in Cali, Colombia was looking for an instructor with a PhD or its equivalent in Mechanical Engineering, to give lectures and work in laboratories as well as coordinate with the other faculty members to set up a new Graduate program, mainly at a master's level. There were no master's degree curricula at that time; only the Undergraduate degrees were offered in various engineering disciplines. I found the opportunity to grow myself, both academically and culturally in a totally new environment in Latin America and learning Spanish, a totally new language for me, very exciting.

After returning from Ottawa, I bought some long-playing records to learn conversational Spanish, and started listening to them in my spare hours, mainly in the evening, and trying to dabble in Spanish. I searched for some Spanish speaking person on campus but couldn't find any. In any case, from July till December, I had enough spare time to get at least some feeling of conversational Spanish and the long-playing records helped. My native tongue Bengali has in its pronunciation sounds like soft T, soft D that English doesn't have, but French has! Thus, Bengali and my very little French helped me in Spanish pronunciation!

Besides, I got busy writing those papers out of my dissertation. A couple of papers were already published in the American journals while I was working on the experimental part. Now, the entire work, including the theory, experiments, and the numerical results needed to be condensed in a synthetic fashion. This was where Professor Hillier helped me through correspondence from Grenoble, France. My good buddies, Jim and Gurnam, were my constant company during those six months. They were also busy with their own doctoral work. Gurnam had to do a lot of experimental work; Jim was lucky in that way. My other friend, Imam Hossain, was also busy; his work was mainly theoretical and computational. Both Pablo and Ildefonso went away years ago; Pablo and Dora were living in Barrie in Northern Ontario, and Ildefonso went back to Monterrey, Mexico, and joined Ford Motor Co. Thus, I had no one to teach me Spanish except the long-playing records!

During my five years at Waterloo, I met some good friends unrelated to my studies. One such family friend was the family of Mr. and Mrs. Wieg with their little son, Olaf. On two occasions in transition, I stayed with them. Hans Wieg and Monika Wieg moved from Germany to Canada in the late fifties when Canada was taking a lot of skilled workers from Europe, especially from Germany and the UK. The Wiegs first settled in British Columbia in a small mining town named Kitimat. After a while they moved to Waterloo, Ontario. Olaf was only nine years old when I met them. When I moved from Kitchener to Waterloo, I stayed with them for a few months. That was when I had already joined the university. I met Mrs. Wieg at the university cafeteria where she worked. From her English accent I guessed that she was from Germany or Austria. I asked her in German: *Sind Sie Deutsche?* (Are you German?). And she was very happily surprised to see a dark-skinned guy asking her in German. From then on, we became good friends, and she invited me to her home to meet her husband Hans and son Olaf. Hans was originally from Hamburg and Monika was from Black Forest. They had totally different accents in German; Hans with his Hamburger Platt-Deutsch and she in her Schwartzwald dialect! And I used to put some of my Swabian words in between while talking with them. They were very simple, unsophisticated people with whom I could spend hours talking about the simple things of life!

When winter became stronger and harder, I moved to a room on University Avenue, just across the train line crossing. It was only a few minutes' walk from the lab where I worked. Also, several of my buddies: Gurnam, Jim and Mr. Mir lived on the same road within a stone's throw from my rented room. Then a room became vacant in the same house where Gurnam lived, and I moved there to be closer to my buddy. The house was owned by a young couple, Mr. and Mrs. Hammermüller and their three little kids: Kurt, Peter and Harry. Harry was a baby when I moved in. I used to have a lot of fun carrying him around all over the house. They lived on the ground floor and there were two extra rooms and a kitchenette in the attic that Gurnam and I used. The relationship with the landlord and the landlady was very friendly. They were Seven Days Adventist by religion and we were invited several times to attend their church meeting on Saturdays. Maybe because of my Indian upbringing I was attracted by their natural way of lifestyle, like vegetarianism, no alcoholic drinks, etc.

When Hans and Monika Wieg bought a house on Smallwood Drive, not too far from the university campus, they asked me to occupy their basement apartment and I moved there at their request and stayed a few months there to have a good family environment. I had been out of my family home in Calcutta for so long, since February 1962 and staying with the Wiegs gave me the warmth of a family environment. In the meantime, Tapas Goswami and Susthir Datta migrated from Germany to Canada. They got jobs in Waterloo and stayed with the Wiegs. There was a time when we three Bengali Indians were living with the Wiegs. Since we all spoke German, it was fun to sit around on the porch on a summer afternoon, drink a few cold beers with warm sausage and bread, prepared by Monika and talk about our years in Deutschland!

Later, I found an apartment for myself, and Imam and I moved there. It was a two-bedroom apartment and had a big living room. We used to have a lot of parties there on the weekends. For the first time we had an apartment of our own, not to share with any family and we wouldn't need permission from any lonesome landlady for mounting our weekend parties! Imam and I lived there till I left for Mexico. Thereafter, Birendra Sahay, another Indian student joined Imam.

I thought that I'd surely miss Imam after leaving Waterloo. We were such good friends! His sister and brother-in-law lived in Arbor, Michigan. He was studying for a PhD in civil engineering at the University of Michigan, a very prestigious school. Imam and I used to visit them a couple of times a year. On the way, Imam would buy his magic equipment in Detroit, and we used to stay overnight in Detroit to have a good time in the evening's pub crawling. Next morning, after a late breakfast or brunch, we would drive to Ann Arbor, only an hour's ride from Detroit. There, in Imam's sister's home we used to have a great family environment, talking and sharing about our whereabouts, all in a Bengali fashion, drinking spiced tea and eating really hot and spicy rice and fish! We used to spend Friday night, the great party night in Detroit, and then Saturday and Sunday with Imam's family in An Arbor, leaving early morning on Monday, returning to Waterloo leisurely by lunch. We used to make just one stop on the way back, either in Windsor or in Hamilton, after crossing the USA-Canada border which used to be quite congested on Mondays.

I must mention that before I left for Mexico, I befriended some people outside my engineering group, in Waterloo. There was a student in the history department, Fe Masonsong from the Philippines who was also a great dancer. She used to participate in our annual celebration of the International Students Union with her Candle Dance of *Binasuan* and *Pandango Sailao,* well-known folk dances of the Philippines. Imam used to show his magic on the same stage, and I met Fe through Imam. Soon Fe finished her master's degree in History and got a teaching position at a High School in Orangeville, Ontario, only an hour's drive north of Waterloo. I remember helping her move to Orangeville with her belongings. I visited her a few times on the weekends. Thereafter I lost touch with her.

There was another student in the language department. She was Gertrud Poppelreiter. I met her at one of our international festivals. Her parents were German, and she spoke German with me. It was good for maintaining my German in practice. In the Chemistry Department, there was Aurora Peñaloza, also from the Philippines. I met her through Dora, Pablo's girlfriend at that time. The four of us used to travel to Toronto on the weekends, first in my old Pontiac and later in Pablo's VW bug. Aurora finished her master's degree in Chemistry and left for USA. Then Dora introduced me to another friend of hers, Michelle, who at that time came recently from France. She was originally from a small town, Wittenheim, bordering Germany. Michelle spoke both German and French fluently. It was a boon for me since I could practice my German and at the same time learn some more French from Michelle. I was also taking some courses in conversational French at Waterloo. Who could be better than Michelle coming straight from France to practice my French? Unfortunately, she went back to Europe, in Switzerland, after a year of training in Canada, and I lost my French teacher!

My two Bengali friends also left Waterloo. Tapas went to Guelph, a small university town very close to Waterloo, within half an hour's drive. He got admission at the University of Guelph (which was an Agricultural College before) to do a Master's degree in Organic Chemistry. Susthir Datta got a job at Spar Aerospace Company, a well-known manufacturing firm in Toronto, and moved there. Our secretary who typed my PhD dissertation would soon be leaving for Victoria in British Columbia for greener pastures. So, most of my friends were leaving Waterloo and I didn't feel too bad in leaving for a new life in Mexico. One fine morning Imam and Ricky drove me to the Lester Pearson International Airport in Toronto. The same goodbye hugs that I was so used to since leaving the Howrah train station in Calcutta on February 12, 1962. I still remember that date.

4

LATIN AMERICA

MEXICO

Cuernavaca was roughly sixty miles from Mexico city's Benito Juarez International Airport. Since the flight from Toronto arrived quite early, I took a public bus to Acapulco, the tourist resort. The bus stopped in Cuernavaca. The journey was very scenic along the winding highway passing through the hills and valleys. The small trees were neatly trimmed in different figures of birds. This was something I had never seen before on an interstate highway in Canada or USA. Reaching Cuernavaca I took another public transportation, a streetcar this time to reach the Intercultural Center of Documentation (Centro Intercultural de Documentación), CIDOC, where we were supposed to registrar for the intensive Spanish course. The place was on the top of a hill, *Rancho Tetela*, overlooking the entire city of Cuernavaca.

It was only 2PM and the line of students still registering gave me a feeling of optimism. There were all kinds of people in the line, boys and girls, young, middle-aged and a bit older as well. At the registration desk I tried my little conversational Spanish that I learned from my long-playing disks in Waterloo. The young girl who was registering me looked up enthusiastically and said: See, you already know some Spanish! I nodded smilingly and she shook my hands: Bienvenido! I got a small single room neatly decorated with simple furniture, a single bed, a small desk and chair and the closet, just like the one at Wolper Hotel when I reached Kitchener-Waterloo, the twin city, some five years ago. At registration they gave a set of study materials, including a thick workbook, a slim writing pad for taking notes, pencil, ball-pen, eraser, etc.

The classes started right away the very next morning at 9AM after breakfast. At breakfast we met a lot of all-new people. The dining hall was humming with different languages, people speaking in full throttle at each table. I sat at a table where I found a man with thick glasses, a bit older than me, and there were two other ladies. One chair was vacant. They were all speaking in English. "May I join you?" I asked politely. "Of course! Please join in!" responded the man in thick glasses. Then I introduced myself as *Jay* and each of them shook hands with me, speaking out their first names. He was Larry, and the two ladies were Cynthia and Merilyn. They all looked like they were in their mid-thirties. He was a lawyer from Chicago. One of the ladies was from England, I guessed from her accent.

Larry and I used to spend our spare time together in the cafeteria of CIDOC or in the small open-air pubs in the downtown of Cuernavaca. Larry's full name was Lorenzo (Laurance) Pozner. His family name was Jewish, and he used to brag that he didn't look Jewish. I didn't know that the Jewish Americans or the American Jews had a special look! Larry was quite an operator. He started dating Cynthia; plus, he had some other "casual" girlfriends, maybe one or two more, all Americans. I used to tease him as "racist" since he would always date American girls. Eventually he seriously fell in love with a Mexican girl and later married her.

Our language classes were very intensive. In the morning, starting at 9AM we had classes in very small groups, each group under a different instructor; all of them were very young in their early or mid-twenties, men and women. Our group of eight students had Alejandro as our teacher. We used to speak aloud from that thick workbook to improve our Spanish pronunciation. The Americans had the problem of pronouncing soft T and soft D, whereas the French, Italian, Portuguese, and even the German and Dutch students (including myself as Bengali/Indian) had no problem at all in pronouncing Spanish T and D. We used to have straight three hours of drilling in the morning. Then lunch at 12 noon and thereafter a *siesta* of two hours till 2 PM. From 2 to 5 we used to have grammar, composition, etc. in bigger groups.

It was around the same time the revolutionary Polish priest, Ivan Illich from New York city moved to Mexico and joined CIDOC. It was a great coincidence of time for me. I heard a lot about the revolutionary activities of Illich, related to Catholic and other religions, but never thought that I'd meet him personally. Illich used to give classes in an open-air environment under the mango trees. This reminded me of the university of *Biswa-Bharati* in Santiniketan, Bengal, India, founded by Rabindranath Tagore. I thought that Illich was a faithful follower of Tagore, as both believed in learning directly from nature.

Illich invited many other leaders of education from the USA and abroad. I have forgotten many of their names but was fortunate to listen to their lectures. Two of them that impressed me very much through their talks were Everett Reimer and Valentina Boreman. Valentina Boreman was a Catholic nun who revolted against many of the rules of the Catholic church and joined the group of Ivan Illich who also happened to be a "revolutionary" Catholic priest from a predominantly Catholic country of Poland. Thus, we had a very revolutionary group of teachers. There was one even all the way from India. His first name was Krishna, a very common Indian name, but I forgot his last name. The other American was the author of the well-known novel "Sons of Sánchez", based on a Cuban family life. Again, I have forgotten the author's name. There were many others who came to give seminars at CIDOC, invited by Ivan Illich. Apart from the language training, those lectures of some of the eminent American thinkers of our time were an extra plus!

Once the three-months crash course was over, Larry and I decided to travel a bit in Southern Mexico, especially to see the famous Mayan temples in Yucatán. Larry had an old Ford Pinto and, of course, I had the free ride. While at Cuernavaca, I took one weekend off to see my good friend Ildefonso in Monterrey, who was one of my buddies at Waterloo. I took a bus from Cuernavaca and then another long-distance luxury bus to Monterrey. The luxury bus even served coffee and warm snacks on the bus. Once I reached Monterrey bus terminal, I found my friend *Ilde* was already waiting there. It was really exciting to see him after several years. We embraced like old friends and then he took me to his home to meet his parents. I stayed with them for two nights. Next day, we went to a party and Ildefonso introduced me to his girlfriend, Margarita.

There were many people at the party, and we had a great time. I was getting a bit self-conscious and shy about my broken, spoken Spanish. I asked Ilde, "Am I doing ok in your language?", and he responded joyfully, "Of course, Jay! What do you think you are speaking, Bengali? You are speaking Mexican Spanish! Just go ahead speaking and don't think right or wrong in pronunciation or grammar!" He, as an old friend, really inspired me to speak without shyness, and I felt good thereafter in participating in their usual party gossip!

Ildefonso had a younger brother who was also with us at the weekend get-together. Their parents, an elderly couple already retired, were extremely nice to me, knowing that Ilde and I were friends at Waterloo. They sent their son, Ilde, to Canada for Graduate studies because they had some reservations about sending him to the USA. Ilde, as a trusted friend of mine, told me that he was planning to marry Margarita. Then he added jokingly, "and then we'll have a few kids!" And that really happened. He invited me to his wedding but by then I was already in South America and couldn't attend his wedding party. Later I came to know that they had a few kids. I'm still looking forward to meeting their kids, but by now probably each one of them has a grown-up family.

Once the Spanish course was done, Larry and I took the long trip to the Mayan empire in Yucatán, making a short one-night stay in Veracruz. Veracruz had a big fishing industry. They fish in the Gulf of Mexico and sometimes stay overnight in the gulf to fish very early in the morning. Larry and I took a trip in the gulf with a group of fishermen, leaving Veracruz very early in the dawn and coming back in the evening. We didn't stay overnight and still they netted a huge amount of a variety of fishes that included red snapper, lobster, and shrimps. Next day we drove along the gulf coast and arrived at Mérida, the state capital of Yucatán. The nearest beach was in *Progreso*, a small tourist attraction, and we got a small hotel there at a moderate rate. We stayed there for a few days but explored the entire Mayan region, from *Chichen Itza* all the way to *Tulúm*. The main temple of Chichen Itza, pyramidal in structure and shape, had a few hundred steps to reach the topmost point. There was a strong steel chain to hold for support while going up. Larry and I didn't need the chain to go up the stairs but took a few pictures just holding the chain. Once we reached the top, wow, a spectacular view of the entire valley with some smaller pyramids around!

After getting down we drove further to visit the Mayan pyramids in Tulúm, about an hour's drive. Interestingly, these were the only pyramids the Mayans built on the coast of Mexico, and that was mainly to protect their empire from the sea pirates that used to pass by along the Gulf of Mexico and the Caribbean Sea en route the Northern coast of South America, mainly Colombia, Venezuela and Guyana. Mayans dominated that entire region that included the current areas of Guatemala and Central America, and even some parts of current Panama and the northern coastal area of Colombia, like the marshland of Chocó, Darien (which is now well known as a stopping spot and a shelter for the Latin American emigrants, mainly from Haiti and Venezuela!) trying to enter Mexico and then to USA. Mayans also influenced culturally the northern areas around today's big cities of Barranquilla, Santa Marta and Cartagena of Colombia. Even in Bucaramanga, there are still traces of the Mayan civilization, particularly in some stone statues in the parks. Bucaramanga is called *La Ciudad de Parques*(the city of parks) for so many municipal parks within the city limits.

Larry and I travelled the whole area of the Mayan domination in Mexico. Then we went to the nearby islands, like Isla de Mujeres, Cozumel, and some others. Getting back to the mainland we drove to the beautiful beach resort area of *Playas del Carmen*, and the surrounding tourist spots. Many years later, I remember, my eldest son Kumar had his wedding party in Playas del Carmen. My good friends from New York City, Imam, and his wife Evie, attended the wedding ceremonies with their daughter Deena! Both Imam and Evie are now no longer with us, but their memories are very bright in my mind. I came to know Imam as a fellow Graduate student at Waterloo in 1965 and then met Evie as his girlfriend in New York where he went to work. The friendship was so strong that they became a part of our extended family. Now their daughter Deena, stays as a part of our family, and she has to take on all the family responsibilities, including her little daughter Lillith, only two years old! Deena herself is only 23!

It took about a week to explore the whole Mayan areas in Yucatán and the surrounding states of México. It was so impressive to see firsthand how powerful the pre-Columbian Mexico was! Not only the Mayans, but also the Aztecs, around the Mexico City and in the Northern and Central Mexico, were incredibly powerful. They dominated even the part of Southern USA, including Texas, New Mexico, Arizona, and Southern California. Both the Mayans and the Aztecs had many branches under numerous names and designations that are described in any history book of pre-colonial Mexico, Guatemala, and Central America.

Once Larry and I returned to Mérida, mainly on the beaches of Progreso, I started communicating with my CUSO head office in Ottawa, Canada, for my next Latin American assignment now that my Spanish language training is done. CUSO asked me when I could leave for Cali, Colombia. I replied: "Right away! Immediately!" I also added that I didn't need to go back to Canada for a week that I was planning earlier. I was more interested to travel directly to Colombia than returning to Waterloo to say goodbye to my buddies like Gurnam, Imam, Jim Thé and others. Both my Latin American friends had left Waterloo long ago; Pablo got a good job with GE Co., Canada, in Barrie, Ontario, and Ildefonso returned to Monterrey, Mexico and got a good position with Ford Motor Company. So, I had no interest in traveling back to Canada. I'd rather move south into the heart of Latin America!

One fine morning I bought my ticket to Cali, Colombia. It was a straight route with only one stopover in Panama City. Larry and I spent a few days partying with our local friends on the Playas of Progresso, and then Larry took me one afternoon to the small airport of Merida. We hugged goodbye. Larry and I had good correspondence while I were in Colombia for two and half years, then in India and again back to London, Ontario, Canada! Then we lost touch, and I don't know where he lived thereafter. The last time when we talked on the phone, some thirty years ago, he told me that he married the Mexican girl he met at Cuernavaca, and that they had a little girl. That girl must be by now a pretty young lady.

CALI, COLOMBIA; KANPUR, INDIA AND LONDON, ONTARIO

My CUSO boss in Colombia was Pierre Beemans from Montreal. Pierre was fluent in French, English and Spanish, and was supervisor of all the CUSO programs in Colombia, Ecuador, Peru, and Bolivia. His girlfriend Teresa was from Bolivia whom he later married. Both are now retired and settled in Ottawa, spending time with their grown grandchildren.

When I reached Cali in May 1970, Pierre fixed me as a paying guest with an young "CUSO-ite" couple, Tom and Claire, both working at the same University Del Valle where I was supposed to start. Tom was in the Math department and Claire was a nurse. They had a little girl, born in Colombia. So, she had dual citizenship: Canadian and Colombian. There were two medical students, Alvaro and Daniel, who lived with the young family of Tom and Claire. We used to have a good family brunch every Sunday. Eventually Alvaro and I became very good friends. Both Daniel and Alvaro were interested in practicing their English with Tom and Claire. It was a very good opportunity for them. But I was interested in practicing my Spanish, and Alvaro found for me a local family to stay with. The family had an extra room and I got that.

Don Luis and Doña Chila were my next "house-hosts". They had several kids, small and grown-up. Their eldest son, Harold, was of my age, and lived with his wife and a little girl in another city, Ibague, in the state of Tolima. Tolima was famous for its typical plate: *Tamales Tolimeses*, very different from the Mexican Tamal that I know. Mexican Tamal is quite hot and rich with spices, as most of the Mexican plates. The second son of Luis and Chila, Omar lived with them with his Swedish wife and a baby daughter. The next son, Raúl lived in the USA with his wife. Thus, the first three "boys" were quite grownups and lived independently. Then came Amparo, the first daughter, who was a teacher and had her own private room. After Amparo, they had two boys, Carlos and Harvey, still in high school; and finally, Iliana and Claudia Patricia, the two end products, were still kids; Iliana was about seven years and Claudia was a baby of three years. It was a big family; and reminded me of some of our joint families in India.

The house was long with a train of rooms for them, then a small patio separating the room and the bath for the maid. Since they had no maid, I got the maid's room and my own private bath! It was a real privilege in such a big family. The house was within walking distance from the university campus. I was paying only for the room and breakfast. I used to have my lunch at the university cafeteria and dinner in some small restaurant outside. Then Doña Chila started feeding me dinner during the weekdays and lunch and dinner on the weekends, sitting around the same table with their entire family. I felt very good being in a family after so many years since I left my own family in India in February 1962! But I didn't want my free eating to continue. I talked with Doña Chila and doubled my monthly rent. Slowly but surely, I felt like a part of their family as if it was my extended family far away from India with my brothers, sisters, and cousins. I started helping Carlos, Harvey and Iliana with their school assignments. Several times I took Amparo out for dinner, and we discussed about her teaching job. We were like brother and sister. With Omar and Marie, I used to talk a lot; their experience in Sweden and Spain and my living in Germany, Canada and Mexico.

At the university, in our Mechanical Engineering Department, there was again an international touch. Two elderly faculty members, Kurt Kerner from Vienna, and Karoly Cherhaty from Budapest were my next-door neighbors in the faculty office quadrant on the second floor of the ME building. Both helped me a lot in settling down with my courses. Like me, both had to learn Spanish as a second or third language, and they could fully realize my challenge of delivering lectures in Spanish in a classroom environment. Then Norman Wilde joined us as another CUSO worker. Norman did his D.Sc. at MIT in Math and was recruited in our mechanical engineering department for helping with the computerized numerical methods that were coming fast with their engineering applications in the early seventies. Norman had several students working in that area. My work was mainly in the Machine Tools and Manufacturing Lab, trying to establish a Graduate program at Master's (M.Sc.) level. There also I got tremendous help from the technicians. Recently, in 2016, when I visited the same university, some of them now retired for many years, came to visit me. One of my ex-students, then a faculty member, came with them. It was, indeed, an indescribable emotion to meet them, hug them and talk to them after so many decades! They came all the way again to our hotel to spend more time with me. My wife was so surprised to see their affection for the old professor they hadn't seen for almost half a century!

There was another faculty member in Civil Engineering, Professor Murphy, with whom I made friends. During early 1972, the university moved from its old campus in the San Fernando area to its brand-new campus in Meléndez, more towards the south of the city after passing the famous champagne-cup shaped Bullfight ring (*Plaza de Toros*) of Cali. Many of us joined together to move our lab equipment safely to the new campus. I remember that Professor Murphy took the lead, and we all followed him as good helping hands. He also helped me personally to pay my yearly ASEE (American Society for Engineering Education) membership fees, since he had a US Dollar account in Colombia. Now I am a Life Member of ASEE after some fifty years of professional membership. This could not have happened unless Professor Murphy had helped me keep continuing my membership in the years of 1970 till 1972!

In Cali, I got acquainted with two fellow Indians. Ram Subramaniam came from the University of Toronto to join us in the Electrical Engineering Department. He, like me and Norman, was also a CUSO worker. Ram was a very pious person and a great practicing yogi. He taught me all the yoga exercises that I still practice today, including the *hatha yoga* postures(*ashanas*), *Pranayama* (breathing exercises) and *Savasana* (posture of cadaver). After completing his two-years assignment at the university, Ram went to the Yogananda Ashram in California, and after a few months of training there, went to Ranchi, India, and joined an ashram there as a *Swamiji*, a Hindu priest dedicating his entire life for the worthwhile cause of helping the country and its workforce in building training centers and programs for the younger *swamis*. After some fifty years, I got connected with him in 2020 through the Internet, thanks to Facebook. Now he is retired, lives in the same ashram quarters and travels to the spiritual spots in the Himalayas and in Tibet. He even invited me to see him in Ranchi during my next visit to India. Once COVID-19 and its current version of Omicron smoothed down, I promised to myself to visit Ram in Ranchi.

My social life in Cali was developed mainly around the family and friends of Don Luis and Doña Chila and their children. I met some young "international" people through Omar and Marie, since they kept good connection with the Europeans, especially from Spain and Sweden, living in Cali. Also, Alvaro was my companion for enjoying a few beers on the weekends. At the university, I had a very good rapport with Miguel Angel Pérez and Germán Cadavid, both from the Agricultural Engineering Department. A couple of times we went to Ibagué with Germán and his wife, where we met Harold, Doña Chila's eldest son. On another occasion, a group of us went to an engineering conference on the Northern coast of Colombia, in Cartagena, a very historic city with its colonial architecture from the Spanish colonial era. In 2019, just before the pandemical problem COVID-19 started, my wife and I went to Cartagena again for another engineering conference. My wife, Matty, was surprised to see the ancient pre-Columbian and the Spanish architectures of the city of Cartagena!

At the University Del Valle, our Mechanical Engineering Chairperson was Claudio Fernández, and the Dean of Engineering was Dr. Alberto León Betancourt. Claudio was a real mechanical engineer, always trying to implement the early computers in solving mechanical engineering problems by numerical methods. Thus, he had a good collaboration with Dr. Norman Wilde and his students. The Electrical Engineering Head of the Department was Guillermo Falk. He studied in Germany, and we used to have a chance to practice our colloquial German whenever we met. We used to meet sometimes at Claudio's home and play cards. Our Dean, Dr. León, used to join us quite often. He was a lonely bachelor, like me at that time, and was in the habit of inviting us for a drink at an open-air restaurant right in front of the university hospital. Miguel Angel and I used to join him every now and then to have some beer and a few shots of Colombian *aguardiente*, a strong and transparent in color local shot.

There was another CUSO worker at the university. She was Barbara (I forgot her last name. No wonder it was over fifty years ago!). She was in the Chemistry Department. Besides Cali, there were other CUSO-ites in other cities of

Colombia. Manfred Fahr was teaching at UIS (Universidad Industrial de Santander) in Bucaramanga. He used to come to Cali a lot, especially during the time of the folk's festival in December: *Feria de Matecañas*. It was during the same festival I met my Ecuadorian friend, Armando Bolivar. In that time huge tents were mounted along Roosevelt Avenue that reminded me of the Oktoberfest in Munich, Germany. In one of those tents while drinking beer, I met Bolivar at one of those long wooden beer tables. After some conversation we became good friends. In later years I helped him to come to Canada to learn English. Gurnam, my buddy, was still there in Waterloo, and Bolivar stayed at Gurnam's place and got admission at a community college to learn English. He stayed there for a year or so, got a certificate for English as a Foreign Language, and then went to Venezuela where I met him again. That was an interesting closing-the-loop of events.

While at Waterloo, Bolivar met a lot of Indians through Gurnam. Some of them lived in the same house and shared the kitchen utensils. They used to clean the kitchen in turn. Once Bolivar cleaned it so spic-and-span that Gurnam called him a great *Karma-yogi!* Bolivar was a very social person and made a lot of Canadian friends, apart from the Indian ones, in his language school, and truly maintained his friendship even after returning to Latin America, this time in Venezuela. When he came to Venezuela I was teaching there, at the Los Andes University in Mérida; and I asked him to stay with me and look for a teaching position, maybe in a high school. That is another story I'll tell later.

By April 1972 I finished my tenure at Del Valle University in Cali, Colombia, and returned to India on a tenured position as an Assistant Professor at the Indian Institute of Technology

(IIT) in Kanpur. At Cali airport, many of my friends and colleagues came to see me off. Don Luis and Doña Chila came with Carlos, Harvey, Iliana and Claudia. I still remember their warm *adios* embrace. They were like my second parents, and they took care of me just like their own son. I used to say Doña Chila: You are my second mother!

After joining IIT Kanpur I stayed a week with my parents in Kolkata. Everyone was very happy on my return after ten years of living abroad in four countries: Germany, Canada, Mexico and Colombia. My friend, Birendra Sahay of Waterloo also joined IIT Kanpur at the same time. In fact, we met on the same flight from New York and after reaching Delhi stayed in the same hotel overnight before leaving for Kanpur. By then he was married and had a baby girl. At Kanpur the academic environment was quite friendly. Moreover, our friend, Dr. Raghubir Sharan, another Waterloo PhD, was already there in the Electrical Engineering Department. He joined IIT a couple of years before us. Raghu's parents were staying with him and his wife, and he used to invite Birendra's young family and me quite often. That way I didn't feel lonely at Kanpur. I was staying at the guesthouse for visitors, and that was good enough for a single man as a starting point for accommodation. Birendra, being a young family man got an apartment. In the meantime, Dr. Rakesh Chawla came from the UK and joined us in the Physics Department. Rakesh was also single and stayed in the same hostel to start with. We were of the same age, both lonely souls, and used to hang around a lot in our spare time. Rakesh bought a car, a VW bug, and we used to go sometimes to the city of Kanpur to get around a bit rather than staying all the time within the IIT campus at Kalyanpur.

The senior faculty at IIT were very friendly with us, the newcomers. That was perhaps due to the international and cross-cultural environment within its campus. We had visiting faculty from America and Europe, as well as tenured professors from all over India. Since all official transactions were in English, there were no provincial language barriers. There were many faculty members from South India whose first language or native tongue were Tamil, Telegu. Malayalam or Canary. Hindi was mainly spoken in Bihar and Uttar Pradesh (UP) plus in many other areas of North India and Madhya Pradesh (MP). In Bengal, Assam and Orissa we had a different group of three languages, Bengali, Assamese and Uria, similar but not same. Within the IIT campus there was absolutely no problem with different languages. Even in social get togethers the language of conversation was mainly English.

Natarajan (Nat) was a friend and fellow Grad student at Waterloo. He worked under Professor Tom Brustowski, and we sometimes shared some measuring instruments for our experimental setups. Nat joined IIT Madras (now Chennai) and later became its Director. Nat's brother, Prabhakaran did his PhD at the prestigious University of Illinois at Urbana-Champagne and joined IIT Kanpur at the same time I joined there. Looked like that the IITs were after the fresh PhDs from North America.

Although there were no language barriers within the IIT campus, there were some discriminations against the non-Hindi speaking people outside the campus, even in Kalyanpur. Once Prabhakaran and I went to the Kalyanpur post office, and he asked for a form. They gave him a form in Hindi. He asked for a form in English and said very politely that he couldn't read Hindi. The postman at the counter was very sarcastic with him and they had a big argument, almost ending up in a fight. I smelled that situation thinking about my future long-term commitment with IIT Kanpur. On a next trip to Delhi where my maternal uncle, the eldest brother of my mom lived, I discussed the Kalyanpur post office incident with him, and he advised me to leave Kanpur and get back to Canada.

I took his advice seriously and started looking for something to support myself in Canada. Finally, and within a very short time, I got an offer to start as a Graduate student in Cultural Geography at the University of Western Ontario and work under Professor Allan Philbrick, a well-known professor of Cultural Geography. His book *Our Human World* was a prescribed textbook that I came to know later. It was a bit odd for a mechanical engineer with a PhD to start studying again in a totally different field like Geography, but I thought that for a short time it would be all right. Besides, the Teaching Assistantship I was offered was good enough to support myself as a single person. In the meantime, I contacted Gurnam, my Waterloo buddy, and he sent me the air ticket. I just vanished from IIT Kanpur and from India without informing anything to anyone, not even my family in Kolkata. Only my uncle in Delhi knew it.

Once I reached Canada and got somehow settled at the University of Western Ontario, I let my family and the IIT authorities know of my departure from India. Both my family and the IIT Director Dr. Muthana were very upset with me. Dr. Muthana asked me to return the money I earned at IIT, which I did. And my family stopped communicating with me for a while. Naturally, they were both very angry with me for my sudden departure without consulting them.

At the other end, I got a very good welcome feeling from Professor Philbrick as well as from his colleagues and

Grad students. Dr. Björklund, his young wife, was also a faculty member in the same department. She became my thesis supervisor, but I stayed with Professor Philbrick as his Teaching Assistant (TA) in an undergraduate course. I was simply helping him on that course and didn't need any special preparation. It was a very different environment than to work as a TA of Professor Pierce at Waterloo where I had to conduct experiments in an Instrumentation and Measurement laboratory in Mechanical Engineering Department!

For living, I shared a two-bedroom apartment with three other Grad students, one from England in the same Geography Department, and two others in Business Administration, one Chinese and the other Canadian. I shared the room with the British student, and he used to give me ride to the school since I had no "old 1954 Pontiac" anymore this time! It was also convenient because we had the same Grad student office in Geography Department. His name was Jefforey. Jeff was a very serious student and had no bad habit like drinking alcohol or smoking pot. He would drink only occasionally a glass of red wine when the four of us used to go out together to dine sometimes on the weekends. The Chinese student had a Philippine girlfriend who would join us now and then to eat together. In the apartment, we shared the kitchen utensils and the refrigerator and never had any problem. Soon Gerald, the Business Administration student finished his MBA, got a job at a bank in Toronto, and left us. Later I met him once in Toronto and had lunch together. He looked much happier, naturally, with a fulltime job than a TA.

I was also taking a couple of Grad courses in the Fall semester of 1972-73 academic year apart from my TA job and had little time to work on a thesis topic. Dr. Björklund was interested in Urban Geography related to the migration of families from farmlands to big cities, attracted by better paid jobs in industries: Pros and cons, promises and problems of such a trend. While I was interested in the topic because I saw in firsthand the same trend in Mexico and Colombia, I had literally no time to work on it. I decided to work on it once the coursework would be complete. Dr. Bjorklund agreed!

On some weekends I would take a ride with someone to the twin cities of Kitchener-Waterloo to see my friend, Tony and Heinz in Kitchener as well as Gurnam Singh and Jim Thé in Waterloo. On a Saturday night, I would go to Schwaben Club with Tony and Heinz to meet Nicky, the bartender and have a great time with them, coming back in midnight to stay at Opa and Oma's place. At other time, I used to go straight to Waterloo to hang out with my buddies and overnight at Gurnam's home. In the meantime, Jim finished his PhD, got a job at the University of Delft, and left for Holland. Dutch was his second language after Aussie English and so there was no language barrier for Jim for teaching and research in Holland. Gurnam was the last to leave Waterloo. Hillier used to joke: Singh is growing roots in Waterloo! Finally, he finished PhD, got a teaching and research faculty position at the University of Moncton, and eventually moved to Moncton in New Brunswick in the eastern part of Canada, near Halifax, Nova Scotia. After returning from his Sabbatical year in France, Professor Hillier also moved to the Memorial University of Newfoundland. Dr. Agnus Bruneau, who was my professor in Materials Science at Waterloo moved to the Memorial University on a high administrative position as the Vice-President and helped Hillier to get a position there. Academia is all family affairs! At Waterloo, upon his return from Grenoble, Hillier was not getting along with Professor Sherburne, the Dean of Engineering, on many research and administrative issues, and Hillier was happy to move out of Waterloo after so many years of tenure.

All my friends and mentors moved out of Waterloo, and I had none to hang out in the weekends, taking a ride from any of the Grad students at Western. London, Ontario was only about sixty miles from Kitchener-Waterloo, almost equidistant from Toronto. *I started feeling lonely for the first time in my life!* Besides, while Cultural Geography was a very interesting and novel field for research, my entire background, both academic and industrial, was in mechanical engineering, and I wanted to get back to my initial and original profession with a regular job. My personal and professional experience over the recent years in Mexico and Colombia were so good that I started looking for another position in Latin America.

In the early and mid-seventies, petroleum price in barrels shoot up manyfold because of the notorious oil embargo in America. Venezuela, the largest oil producing and exporting country in the American continents, both North and South, was booming in its economic growth. So, I contacted the Venezuelan Embassy in Ottawa for an academic position at one of their universities. They responded very quickly, asking for all my academic and industrial transcripts, duly attested by a notary public of the provincial Government of Ontario. I did it equally quickly and sent all my papers to them. In a week the response came that the University of Los Andes in Mérida, Venezuela is looking for a faculty member for teaching, research, and service in its newly formed Mechanical Engineering Department. I immediately agreed to try for the position and requested the Venezuelan Embassy to mail all my attested transcripts to the Chairperson, Mechanical Engineering Department, University of Los Andes, Mérida. Parallelly. I wrote a forwarding letter with another xerox copy of my attested credentials, addressing it to the same Chairperson of Mechanical Engineering Department. If for some reason the Embassy failed to dispatch my transcripts on time, at least the ones sent directly to the ME Chairperson by me would arrive on time. I wrote the cover letter in Spanish!

In a surprisingly short time, within three weeks, I got a letter from Professor Nestor Joussef, the Mechanical Engineering Chair, offering me a tenure-track position as an Assistant Professor, the same rank I had in Colombia. I was elated with joy! Later, when we eventually became reliable colleagues and confidential friends, he told me that he received around that time many applications, each was stating the applicant's good working knowledge in Spanish, but I was the only one who actually wrote the letter in Spanish. I remembered what my Jewish German teacher in Calcutta use to say: *Übung macht den Meister!*

I had to tell Professor Philbrick and Dr. Björklund about my job offer in Venezuela. They understood my position and happily agreed unconditionally to my resignation as a Grad student and as a TA. Professor Philbrick gave me an affectionate pat on the back with his usual smile and added: When you come to Canada, don't forget to visit us. We'll still be here.

I broke the news to my roommates Jeff and Chang. They were a bit disappointed, for Gerald had already left for Toronto and I would be leaving soon. They had to find two more roommates to share the rent of a costly two-bedroom apartment. Nevertheless, I spent most of the summer semester of 1973 with them while traveling a few times to Waterloo. Gurnam was still there since his appointment at the University of Moncton would also initiate in Fall 1973. Dr N. K. Srivastava, another Waterloo PhD in Civil Engineering, was already at Moncton. Gurnam would probably get some help from him in the earlier stages of settling down. This time with a steady job he wouldn't have any problem even if he wanted "to grow roots there", as Hillier used to say for pulling his leg.

This time through Gurnam Singh, I met two Indian Professors at Waterloo, one in Mathematics and the other in Statistics. Dr. Murthy in the Math department was of our age and used to drop by at Gurnam's place for an occasional tea in the afternoon. His expertise was in Combinatorial Methods. Like Jeff at Western, Murthy was also a nonsmoker and alcohol-free guy, much devoted to spiritual thoughts, both in theory and practice. Professor Godambe, the Statistician, was a real cool person, roughly about ten to fifteen years senior to us. In 1973, I was 33; he must have been at that time in his late forties or early fifties. He was very famous worldwide for his original research in Estimation Function in Statistics and in the other allied areas of theoretical statistics. His established research area had wide applications in Game Theories, Stock Markets, Insurance companies (Actuaries), even in industrial mass production of goods and services. He was single, living in a single-bedroom apartment very close to the university campus. He lived a very simple life but loved to drink beer and eat fish!

Professor Godambe used to accompany Gurnam and me during the weekends for pub hopping. Sometimes he would join us in Circus Room where the artists and art fans of Waterloo used to hang out. He loved music and dance. We would take him to Schwaben Club on some Saturdays, and he became good friends with Tony and Heinz there. Once the music started, he would approach a table very cheerfully and ask a girl to dance. Usually, in Schwaben Club no single girl would refuse to dance with an unknown person, a stranger, because that was the real fun to dance with a new face and chat while dancing. There was literally no discrimination in Schwaben Club. Saturday evenings used to be very alive with music and dance.

It was hard to accept such a famous statistician as Professor Godambe, academically equivalent in the rank of Prof. P. C. Mahalanabis, founder of the famous journal of Statistics, *Sankhya,* and Prof. Rao, was so humble. There was another Indian statistician, Dr. J. N. K Rao, also quite well-known in the field of Biostatistics. Professor Godambe used to joke with a mock-rivalry, referring to J.N.K Rao as *"Junky"* Rao. It was not serious, just for teasing!

In the meantime, our friend Imam Hossain got a good offer in the famous bridge design engineering firm Amman & Whitney in New York. He was in the final stage of his PhD dissertation, but the offer was so attractive that he could not resist the temptation. He arranged mutually with his supervisor, another British professor, to come back later to finish up and defend the final oral examination, the notorious *Viva Voce* for a doctoral candidate. Next year he took a short leave from his job, came to Waterloo, stayed with our common friend Gurnam, wrote the thesis, and defended it successfully and became Dr. Imam Hossain! Gurnam helped him in his English write up. Gurnam helped many other Indian students in writing their theses. No wonder he took so long to write his own!

While Imam was in NYC, Gurnam, Professor Godambe and I went to visit him. We drove all the way, riding in Godambe's big Impala. Both Gurnam and I changed hands since Godambe was a very careless and lousy driver; we couldn't take a chance with him behind the wheel. It was a very joyful trip. We stopped for lunch and then coffee cum snacks wherever we wanted to fill the tank. The weekend traffic was very slow due to the usual highway congestion on a Saturday, especially at the Canada-USA borders. We reached Imam's apartment at around 9PM. He said: My girlfriend was waiting so long to meet you guys! She just left. Gurnam coolly replied, as always, "Wow, Imam, you have a New Yorker girlfriend! Don't worry, be happy! We'll see her tomorrow!" "What do you guys expect? In New York I'll get a shy Indian girl?" Imam replied spontaneously. He and his girlfriend prepared food for us: Basmati rice with nuts and spice (Pulao), lentil dal, fish curry and Bengali sweets! We ate with full delight, drank a few beers with our usual gossip – talk of the town – stretching out on his living room sofas. We three had a sound sleep till late the next Sunday morning. We were dog-tired from the long journey of some six hundred miles from Waterloo to NYC!

Sunday afternoon Imam's girlfriend Evelyn came. A slim girl of medium height, roughly about 5 ft 4 inches, just right for Imam, I pondered. We all went to Greenwich village, a great attraction for young people like us to spend the evening. It was summer and there were lots of pedestrians, and many tourists. At the end of our long walks seeing different art galleries and stores, we finally settled down at a sidewalk restaurant for our dinner. So many people of all colors are passing by with giggling talks. You really could feel the mood of summer in New York City. We took the train to get back to Imam's place, relaxed a bit with some more drinks. Then Evelyn took the train again to get back to her home.

From that day on till today Evelyn became a good family friend to all of us. From her conversations that evening, I found her to be a very open-minded and simple person. She was a professional in fine arts and still paints on canvas. We are fortunate to have her now as a family friend. Only a few days back Evelyn joined us in a family video-chat, a virtual get-together celebrating the 75th birthday of my ex-wife. She is also the godmother of our youngest son, Nayan. We were remembering those good old days when our kids were toddlers and babies and how Imam and Evelyn used to take care of them on our visits to New York. That is another story I'll tell later.

On Monday morning, we said goodbye to Imam because he had to go to work, and we left New York on our way back to Waterloo, Canada, leaving nice memories of a busy but very rewarding weekend behind. Taking the same route back we reached Waterloo again late in the evening. Godambe's apartment building was right in front of Gurnam's house right across the road. On the way, after crossing the USA-Canada border we had a good dinner in a French/Quebecer restaurant with delicious chicken in spicy creole sauce, long fries and, of course, some cold beer for relaxing from a longish trip. Reaching Godambe's building we put back carefully his car in its proper parking, as Godambe always loved to use the word "proper" as a good statistician. We walked back to Gurnam's place and slept right away.

This time during my relatively shorter stay in Canada, only a year, from August 1972 till August 1973, I happened to meet a variety of people from different walks of life. Prithvi Pal and Hardev Singh lived in the basement of Gurnam's house. Both were very hardworking truck drivers. They were both from Punjab in Northwestern India. Gurnam lived on the second floor with his nephew Amarjit. Amarjit was a factory employee in a manufacturing firm. Gurnam and Amarjit were single souls without any family responsibilities.

Prithvi Pal and Hardev had their families in India, and their families were waiting for the immigration visa for landing in Canada. There were occasions when five of us would sit together to eat Punjabi food with chapati, dal and delicious raita prepared by Prithvi Pal. Hardev was a quiet person, but Prithvi Pal used to enlighten us with his stories during our dinner time.

Many things had changed since I left Waterloo for Mexico in January 1969 and my return trip from Colombia and India in September 1972, close to three years. I went to visit Hans and Monika Wieg. They were both retired and lived a quieter life in their same home they bought on Smallwood Drive. Olaf, their son, got married and moved out. He has a baby boy named Keenen. Olaf came with little Keenen to visit his parents. To me it was a great joy to see Olaf again whom I knew as a much younger adult when I first moved to their home as a paying guest in late 1964. Now Keenen is taking Olaf's space in their small family. He is only a year old but very active like his grandma Monika. Every time I see Mrs. Wieg, she reminds me of my own mother whose name was also Monika.

At Western Ontario, in the Department of Geography there were other senior faculty members, colleagues of Professor Philbrick. Professor Warntz was originally from the University of Chicago but moved to Canada as a protest against the US involvement in Vietnam and the Vietnam War during the late sixties and early seventies. His expertise was in Theoretical Geography. Professor Packer was from the UK. He was in Urban Planning. Professor Philbrick was originally from farmland in Maine but worked in Utah. Dr. Björklund was his second wife and much younger to him. When I met them, he was in his mid-sixties, and she was in her late forties. Among the younger faculty members there was Dr. Jenelle, the Graduate Officer who used to take care of the administrative issues of the Graduate students. He was a very sweet person, always in a jolly good mood. Then, there was Dr. Terry Smith from England. For his very long flying hair we used to call him "hippie professor". He was very young, perhaps the youngest of all the faculty members in the geography department. He was married to an African American and they used to come together quite often to our Grad. parties. Terry was very interested in mathematical modeling. Knowing that I am an engineer, he used to come to me for consulting on mathematical issues and wanted to offer me a Research assistantship (RA) to work with him. But I was better off under Professor Philbrick and Dr. Björklund.

Among the Grad students in Geography, there were Allan Swami and Steve Ali from Trinidad and Tobago. They were very interested in playing cricket and formed a team with the students and teachers from India, England, Pakistan, Sri Lanka and Australia. The campus had in fact a cricket field for us to play. There were two Canadian students I got befriended with. One was of a very slim and short structure, almost of my height, 5 ft 4 inches. He was very interested in traveling to Latin America and I used to inspire him with my stories of Mexico and Colombia. I came to know that later after finishing his master's degree he moved to somewhere in South America. Another Canadian was a very tall and hefty personality, who used to tell us a lot of jokes aloud on Canadian politics. He was from Waterloo and used to go home at the weekends. He always gave me a ride to Waterloo whenever I wanted. On the way we would stop somewhere to grab a sandwich and a beer. We used to treat each other every alternate week. The drive from London, Ontario to Waterloo was about an hour and half. We used to talk about all kinds of university politics, always with a twist of his jokes.

Among my Indian friends who came from Biberach, Germany to Waterloo, and stayed in the basement room in the Smallwood Street home of Hans and Monika Wieg, Susthir moved to Toronto and Tapas joined the University of Guelph as a Graduate student for a master's degree in Chemistry. I had a distant cousin in Hamilton. Her husband, Dr. Rajat Bhaduri was a professor of Physics at McMaster's University. When Imam and I shared an apartment, they used to come sometimes with their two little kids. We could speak with them in our native tongue, Bengali. Besides, Imam's friend from back home in East Pakistan, now Bangladesh, Saukat Ali and his wife Babu came a couple of times from Toronto. Saukat was doing a PhD at the University of Toronto and Babu got a job in a department store. They were a happy couple but didn't have any children. I remember that Babu used to criticize the mess in our bachelor's apartment and our disorganized bachelor's life. She was very enthusiastic that both of us, Imam and I, would start our family life, getting married rather than fooling around with our girlfriends, because she somehow felt that we wouldn't marry them. She even once tried to arrange a marriage interview for me with a Bengali girl in Toronto. But it didn't work!

This was all about my short stay for the second time in Canada. At least I got reconnected with my buddies, Gurnam and Jim Thé and made some new friends like Professor Godambe and Prithvi Pal. This time Gurnam and Jim accompanied me to the Toronto International airport. It was an American Airlines flight to Caracas, Venezuela with a brief stopover in New York. Again, the same departure hugs! The last time they were from Imam and Ricky, this time from

Gurnam and Jim. Before entering the check-in area, I turned around to look back and they waved their hands high in the air! I heard from a distance: Bon voyage, Jay!

MÉRIDA, VENEZUELA

The University of Los Andes (ULA) in Mérida sent me the air ticket all the way from Toronto to Mérida but I wanted to see firsthand the beautiful sceneries of the prairie plains and the Andes mountains from Caracas to Mérida that I had seen so far on the colorful pictures and intercontinental maps of the Americas. The plane landed a little after 12 noon and I took a free transport bus from the Simon Bolivar International airport to the central bus terminus in Caracas. Then I took a long-distance bus right away from Caracas to Mérida. The first stop was in Valencia through an eight-lane highway, very well-maintained, no less in quality than any interstate highway in the USA or Canada. I tried some typical Venezuelan *"arepa"* with cheese, famous *"Queso Guayanés"* and ham. An arepa in Venezuela and Colombia is so filling that it could easily be a full breakfast, lunch or dinner in American standard. After Valencia the bus roared in high speed through the plains of the prairies passing by the cities of Acarígua, Guanare and Barínas, with splendid green flatlands on both sides. Then the bus started climbing up on a narrower, serpentine road, also called a "highway" "Autopista" or "Carretera vial principal" in Spanish. The scene from above in the mountain, looking down on the deep green prairies was spectacular. As the bus started climbing up and up the weather started changing as well. It was getting colder and relatively much drier than in the plains. The topmost point was really cold, even for me living in Canada. There was a huge statue with an eagle on its top. The Venezuelans say that the face of the eagle looks like the face of Simon Bolivar, the liberator of five Latin American countries and the founding father of the sixth one: Bolívia. Hence, the place is called *Pico Bolivar*. Thereafter the bus slowly started descending again down the winding road and stopped at a gas station that had a small shop attached where people eat and drink something. I took a couple of shots of the local schnaps, very strong but crystal clear. I was joking with the person who was sitting beside me all the way from Caracas. I told him: If I drink two more, the winding road will fall straight in my vision. He laughed his head off. Probably he heard this joke for the first time!

After two hours on that winding road, we reached Mérida, and a typical mountain breeze woke me up after those two shots of "aguardiente". I had a reservation at a small hotel near the University campus. I still remember; it was right across the very impressive administrative building of the university, a tower of ten floors. By the time I reached my hotel it was already dark. From Caracas to Mérida, it takes about ten to twelve hours depending on the weather conditions on the mountainous roads. I was tired, traveling from Toronto with a stopover and plane change in New York and without any rest in Caracas. I just went to bed. The arepa in Valencia helped me in not eating any dinner or even any evening snacks.

But the next morning I woke up early and had my breakfast right in the hotel. Scrambled eggs with toast, freshly brewed orange juice with no ice in it and coffee. It was just right, both in quantity and quality, for breakfast quite early in the morning. Then I went up to my room to read the morning daily to get around with the local whereabouts. At 9PM I got a call from the receptionist that someone from the university was waiting in the lobby to see me. I went down and a very dark, tall and fattish gentleman came forward and introduced himself as Professor Miguel Arcángel Rada. I introduced myself with my short name Jay (rather than Jayanta) Banerjee. We sat down on a sofa and Miguel gave me some ideas about the School of Mechanical Engineering (not a department!): number of faculty members, student strength, class lectures, etc. He also explained that the school had three different but interrelated departments: Mechanical Design, Materials and Manufacturing, and Thermal Sciences. I was supposed to work in Mechanical Design as well as in Materials and Manufacturing Department. That sounded to me very reasonable, since Materials Science links with both Design and Manufacturing Engineering. For example, Tribology (which includes the science and technology of friction, wear and lubrication in mechanical systems) is involved very closely with design as well as manufacturing.

After a while Professor Rada took me to our Engineering Faculty which was only a couple of blocks from my hotel, and we just walked. There Miguel took me first to the Chairperson /Director of the ME School, Professor Néstor Joussef, a short person with a few gray hairs and slim figure with no beer belly. He shook my hand warmly with an inviting smile and said: *Bienvenido,* Dr. Banerjee. We entered his office and after a few minutes Professor Rada left. Professor Joussef gave me, more or less, the same information that Miguel already mentioned. Then he took me around to show the labs of Materials, Manufacturing, Thermal Sciences and Design. Most of the labs had equipment; for example, the materials lab had several optical instruments, a tensile testing machine and some other measuring instruments. The manufacturing lab had many general-purpose machine tools, like lathe, milling machine, radial drill and a flat surface grinder. Only the design lab had no instruments but a few long tables and drawing boards. In 1973 there were no PCs (Personal Computer)!

Professor Joussef told me that there was an apartment where a young faculty member, Rafael Molina, lived and there was a vacant room if I wished to share. I immediately agreed, reflecting on my lovely experience of living with the family of Don Luis and Doña Chila in Colombia. Later, on the same day after showing me the campus on a walking tour and introducing me to the Dean of Engineering, he took me in his small car, am American Chevette, to my hotel and I checked out. Looked like that he had already talked with Rafael Molina and was only waiting for my decision. The apartment was on the third floor of a small building, not too far from the engineering faculty, and the building had a narrow elevator, good enough for 3 or 4 persons to ride together.

Professor Joussef knocked at the entrance door and a slim and tall guy opened it with a smiling face. Professor Joussef introduced me to him and again I got a warm handshake from Rafael. They both accompanied me to show my room, and Rafael handed over to me two keys: one for the apartment and the other for the main entrance of the building. No, there were no key for the individual room to lock it from inside or outside. I didn't feel uncomfortable for this so-called lack of privacy, since I had no personal room key, neither in Colombia nor in Canada. Three of us sat down leisurely in the living room, not too large but quite comfortable with two sofas and a central low table for coffee and snacks. The apartment also had a small kitchen for cooking small things and some utensils. It was a typical bachelors' apartment. I was quite happy to have my own room. That was all I needed to start living in a new environment again! By now I am used to it.

After Professor Joussef left, I unpacked my very limited belongings in my "private" room, put them in the "proper places" (as Professor Godambe at Waterloo would add!). Then Rafael and I sat down in the living room, both in a very relaxed mood and exchanged information mainly about ourselves: our families and friends, our previous jobs and other experiences related and unrelated to our work. Rafael had another brother, Fidel who was still in high school in San Cristóbal, a nearby city in the adjacent state of Táchira. After our initial conversation I took a cat-nap in my room and then Rafael invited me for a popular dinner of rice and black beans *(caraotas)* plus meat at a restaurant plus beer parlor, called *Tú y Yo,* right in front of our apartment building. While dining we talked again about the University of Los Andes (ULA) and its School of Mechanical Engineering. The school was relatively new and small with about fifteen faculty members and no Graduate program yet. Three schools of engineering started operating only a year back: Mechanical, Chemical and Systems Engineering. Professor Joussef came from Maracaibo, the big Petropolis of Venezuela, to become the Founding Director of Mechanical Engineering at the University of Los Andes (ULA) in the historic city of Mérida, Venezuela!

Next morning Rafael took me to our ME School and introduced me to several faculty members. Some of them were quite young, Rafael's contemporary, and graduated with him from the University of Zulia (La Universidad de Zulia, LUZ) in Maracaibo. Professor Joussef was a faculty member there and when he moved to the University of Los Andes (ULA) as the Founding Director of Mechanical Engineering, he brought his favorite ME graduates with him. Later on, I became a good friend of my director and of another faculty member, Professor Roberto Suárez, roughly my age. Roberto and I shared an office room together for several years. Roberto studied in Poland and his wife, Zófia, was Polish. Roberto and I shared not only our office space but also our spare time, conversing on many topics other than mechanical engineering while dining together in some local cafeteria or in small pub, drinking beer of the local trademarks *Polar* or *Zulia*.

I started giving classes on Machine Tools and adding new teaching experiments in a manufacturing lab, the kind of work I did before in Colombia. The idea was to improve the lab and to make it adequate for inclusion in a master's degree program. Professor Joussef was a very enthusiastic and active personality, always thinking with a positive mind. There was another faculty member in the area of Metallurgy and Material Science, Professor Parada. Parada studied in México, at the Universidad Nacional Autónoma de México (UNAM) and his wife was Mexican. Thus, with Roberto and Parada, I had an international academic and socio-cultural environment around me. We three used to hang around a lot, especially in the evenings in some local pub, drinking, criticizing the present politics worldwide or simply gossiping on the local whereabouts.

In the meantime, Bolivar, my Ecuadorian friend, whom I met at the *Feria de Matecañas* in Cali three year ago, came back from Canada after finishing his courses in English and joined me. Rafael's brother Fidel finished high school and started at our university in Physics. Rafael moved to a different apartment in the same building with his brother, and I invited Bolivar to stay with me in Rafael's vacant room. Again, two old friends, Bolivar and I, started enjoying our stay together, sharing food and cooking, laundry and our spare time. I introduced him to Roberto, Miguel Rada, Parada and our boss Professor Joussef. We had a great group for gossiping on world affairs! Bolivar got a job to teach at a local high school. After the Christmas and New Year holiday season, local fairs start just like in Colombia. There was the *Feria del Sol* in Mérida where a lot of tourists used to come from all over Venezuela and Colombia. Then started *Feria de San Sebastián* in San Cristóbal, Táchira, the next state adjacent to Mérida. Driving time between Mérida and San Cristóbal by local transportation, small bus or shared taxis, was about three hours.

On one weekend, Bolivar and I decided to go to San Cristóbal to spend time at the Feria de San Sebastián and then cross the border to *Cúcuta* in Colombia, thus seeing the two countries in the long weekend, hitting two birds with one stone! We went to the bus terminal of Mérida and found a shared taxi. We got into the taxi and took the two front seats beside the driver. The back seats were still vacant. Suddenly three young ladies jumped into the backseats. The cab was full, and we were ready to leave for San Cristóbal. Presumably, we were all going to the San Sebastián's country fair! Bolivar was sitting right beside the driver, and I squeezed myself beside him. Thus, we were three of us, including the driver, in the front seats of the car and three young girls in the back seats. As soon as we started Bolivar turned his head back, greeted the girls very gently, *Buenos Días,* and asked: Are you going to see the fair in San Cristóbal? The girl in the middle seat, with long black hair and slightly tanned skin, replied enthusiastically, "Yes, we are all going to the feria of San Sebastian. Are you?" Bolivar replied with equal enthusiasm in his voice, "Yes. we too are going there! We will be staying in San Cristóbal over the weekend and return to Mérida on

Monday afternoon." I wondered why the hell he was giving so much details of information to people we hardly knew. Anyway, Bolivar started a conversation in his style. The girl sitting behind the driver's seat was very silent. She was sitting exactly diagonally across from me and I could see her just by turning my head a bit backward to the left. She had short hair painted in a light crimson color. And she had round Gandhi-style sunglasses on. Bolivar was speaking about his experience in Canada. I felt that he was telling his story with genuine interest in convincing the long-haired girl to keep some connection in future. He was also elated to speak on his Canadian experience in his own language fluently rather than in English. The conversation became very lively as the girl in the middle seat started asking questions about the touristic places, the people, and their lifestyles in Canada. Bolivar explained how beautiful it was to see Niagara Falls from the Canadian side rather than from the US side across the border. The short-haired girl behind the driver was still silent! To pass time, Bolivar told his favorite jokes. I had heard them many times from him, especially after a few drinks at parties.

We had a winding road descending from the mountains around Mérida to the plains of *El Vigia*. It took about an hour and half. The cab stopped at a gas station to fill up the tank and we all went to the adjacent cafeteria to fill us up a bit with coffee. By now my friend Bolivar was much friendlier with the long-haired girl. All five of us got out of the cab and entered the cafeteria. It was only a twenty-minute stop-over time. So, we quickly ordered coffee and small pastels (*pastelitos*) for snacks. Bolivar paid for himself and for the long-haired girl. When I wanted to pay for the short-haired girl who was eating standing by my side, she refused my invitation with a very polite smile: Thank you, but I'd like to pay for myself.

We got back into the car and left immediately. The driver was already waiting at the pump. Now he could drive much faster on the straight and much wider highway on the prairies, passed by *La Fria*, another small town and reached San Cristóbal in an hour. As we left the cab, Bolivar tried to get some contact phone numbers of the girls. He didn't succeed! They vanished into the crowd of the busy bus terminal, and we took our own way, settling in a small hotel near the bus station. We went up to our room on the second floor, freshened up a bit and headed to the fairground, thinking that we could probably find the girls there. No luck! We took several rides on the merry- go- around, tunnels and other entertaining lifting machines, but nowhere could we find our cab companions from Mérida. Brokenhearted we went to Cúcuta in Colombia and stayed there on Sunday night in another small hotel, spending the evening in a very entertaining nightclub.

Monday very early in the morning we got back to the same bus terminus in San Cristóbal to get again a shared cab ride back to Mérida; and to our great surprise we saw the same two girls – the longhaired and the shorthaired - waiting for a taxi. It was really a miraculous coincidence that I still cannot grasp logically! Life is a coincidence!

They had no idea about where we went, nor did we know about their whereabouts! On the way back, another Peruvian lady, a bit older than us, took the third seat in the back. She was quite talkative and both Bolivar and she entertained the entire trip back to Merida. The cab stopped again at the same gas station in El Vigia and we four entered the same cafeteria for coffee and pastels. This time the short-haired girl accepted my invitation! As we reached Mérida, Bolivar again tried his best to get a contact number of them, but alas no luck again, and they vanished in the crowd of the busy bus station. We got back to our apartment utterly disappointed. We couldn't even get the names of them.

In February there was a birthday party for a professor of the History department. He was a great friend of *Anusuya*, an Indian professor in the English department. I came to know Anusuya in a previous get-together of the new faculty members. Bolivar and I talked with Anusuya, and we decided to throw the party in our apartment. I had a record player and a few long-playing disks, good enough for a small party. I also invited three of my most favorite students: Ricardo Murillo, Juan Briceño and Rigoberto Reinoza. I still remember their names! Anusuya also invited some of her friends, including a young military captain from the Indian army who was just visiting her.

In the morning, Bolivar and I went to the grocery store on the ground floor of the same building where we were living as we wanted to buy some snacks and some booze for the party in the evening. The grocery store was quite large, almost the size of a small department store with its parallel passages and isles, rest rooms and a small cafeteria. We were picking up things and putting them in the shopping cart, turning from one isle to another for the drinks, and at one turn from one row of drinks to another we faced right in front of us, almost bumping into them, those two girls, the short-haired and the long-haired, who traveled on the same shared taxi with us to the San Sebastian Folkfest in San Cristóbal a few weeks ago. Bolivar and I were spellbound! Another coincidence! Maybe they were shocked too to see us so unexpectedly. Anyway, after the usual exchange of greetings, Bolivar told them that in the same evening we were planning a party to celebrate the birthday of a history professor and we had invited some other professors and a few students. Instead of keeping silent, I added: You two are most cordially invited. The long-haired asked: At what time? Bolivar replied enthusiastically: Come by at around seven. The short-haired nodded affirmatively, and for the first time she smiled at me. In reply, I pointed at our apartment building, and added: It is right here in this building! Remember, apartment number five. She smiled again. Then with a brief *adios* they turned towards a different row of food racks.

With our groceries Bolivar and I went back to our apartment and were busy cleaning the living room and the kitchen. I asked him: "Do you think that the girls will show up at our party? "For sure!" he put an extra emphasis on the word *sure*. Bolivar was always very optimistic. No wonder he went all the way from Ecuador to Canada for some English courses! After cleaning the apartment, we arranged the paper plates and the plastic utensils in their respective cupboards and cut the cheese, sausages, ham, etc. into small pieces. The munchies would be served in the form of cold snacks plus some fresh bread to put them on and thus avoid any cooking during the party. This was again Bolivar's great idea. He had more experience than me in throwing parties, especially in a Latin American cum Caribbean culture. After finishing cleaning, we both took a short nap to stay awake in good shape late in the evening.

People started coming after six o'clock. First, some of my students came. Then came Anusuya with a big birthday cake. The young Indian captain, Arun, came with her. After a short interval came the History professor, the birthday baby! I also invited my boss Professor Néstor Joussef and my good friend Roberto. People started coming slowly one by one and we put the music and the booze in circulation. My two faithful students, Ricardo Murillo and Juan Briceño, helped in serving the drinks and the snacks. With music and conversations, the party was warming up. I lost hope of our two lady invitees to arrive, and asked Bolivar, "What do you think? Will the girls come?". And with the same tone of affirmative confirmation he replied, "For sure!" Again, what a coincidence! At that very moment there was a mild knock at the door. I opened it with my usual nervousness, and there stood the two invitees right in front, the short-haired and the long-haired *señoritas*! I kept the door wide open for them as a sign of welcoming greetings, bowed my head a little in Asian style and they entered.

My two students were busy entertaining the guests with drinks. Bolivar raised the volume of music and lowered the lights. People started dancing. Anusuya started dancing with the History professor, Arun with our long-haired invitee, Roberto with Sofia and so on. My good friend Bolivar was getting a bit annoyed as Arun continued dancing with the long-haired one. I assured Bolivar: Arun is just on a visit from India and, moreover, he is with Anusuya; so, you don't need to worry." Finally, with my usual hesitancy, I asked the short-haired one to dance, and she agreed! Slowly, she got up from her chair. I felt great! By now Bolivar and I had met them three times, and we didn't even know their names. Maybe Bolivar already knew but didn't tell me, I pondered. While dancing I asked her politely: What is your name? She smiled again and replied softly: *Eligia*. I felt confident in myself and continued, "And what is your friend's name?" "Laddy" she replied with a short smile again.

The party was going on smoothly with occasional jokes and laughter with softer background music for closer dances. Everyone was in a good mood. Finally, Arun sat down, and Bolivar got Laddy for dancing! I was relieved to see my friend dancing. We also arranged for some simple food to be delivered from a local catering rather than cooking at home. The food came at around ten and we all sat down in our chairs with the paper plates on our laps. We had no dining table! Also, we used simple plastic cutlery. This was our first party in our bachelor's apartment, and we had no elaborate dining arrangements. The most important part was to get together with friends. And that part was totally satisfactory with good music and dance that was not planned *a priori*. While eating, the background song was still going on: *¡Besame mucho como si fuera esta noche la última vez! ¡Qué tengo miedo de perderte, perderte otra vez!*

People slowly started getting up to leave before midnight. Roberto and Zófia left first. Then Anusuya, the history professor and Arun got up. I asked Ricardo and Juan to stay around so that Bolivar and I could give a ride back to Laddy and Eligia. Eligia was staying overnight with Laddy's family. By then I had bought a little British car, *Hillman*. Bolivar and I gave them a ride in my little car, and that was the first time Bolivar and I had some company in our car. They lived not too far on the other side of the university campus, only about ten minutes' drive from our apartment. As they got out of the car, we thanked them for coming and they thanked us for being such hospitable hosts!

The Hillman I bought had its own history. One day in our faculty lounge we were eating lunch and gossiping over the talk of the town. One young faculty member, Rafael's friend Oswaldo, was talking about the cars and their new arrivals. I got interested and Oswaldo took me to a dealer right across our campus. They showed several foreign models and the moderately inexpensive one was the British made *Hillman*. It was about three thousand US Dollars at the exchange rate of the Venezuelan currency, also called *Bolivar,* my friend's name (1USD = 4.3Bs was the exchange rate in 1973 and stayed steady till 1982!). I had that money saved from my earlier jobs, and I bought the car with full payment in cash. It was small, but quite comfortable for four passengers! The size was similar to that of a VW, Fiat or Renault. It was light yellow in color. Once I had a vehicle to move around, Bolivar and I used to drive around within the city limits of Mérida but not yet on the typically narrow highways of the Andes mountains around Mérida.

Later, we started to drive around with Laddy and Eligia in my little Hillman. We came to know Laddy's parents, brothers and sisters. Eligia's parents lived in Valencia, near Caracas, and she had room and board with a neighboring family in Mérida. One day we invited Laddy's brothers, Miguelito and Milton, to have a British style High Tea with us. Actually, tea was not very common in Venezuela; so, we had coffee and cakes. Bolivar, being from Ecuador, was an expert in brewing coffee and I brought the cakes from a nearby bakery. Apparently, after that afternoon *high tea*, both the brothers were happy to see our dwelling place and gave us the green light to invite their sisters out. Eventually, we were also invited to their home by Laddy's parents, a soft-spoken elderly couple who accepted Bolivar and me as good and trustable young *gentlemen* as their daughters' friends. From then on, we could invite Eligia and Laddy for an afternoon coffee or for an evening movie.

One morning in a weekend we decided to take the car out on the narrow highway outside Mérida. It was a bright day and we invited Eligia and Laddy to come along with us. We got out of Mérida and decided to drive further up on the mountains towards *Mucuchies*, as I remembered the town on my first trip from Caracas to Mérida. There were many small towns on the way from Mérida to Mucuchies: Mucubají, Mucurbá, Mucujún, etc. *"Mucu"* means *"home"* in the local Amerindian language. After driving an hour, we found a plane, grassy area on the side of a creek. We parked the car in the plane area, nice, clean, and green, and spread the blanket that I always carried in my car. We sat and spread out some sandwiches and sodas we brought with us. After finishing eating, we went around for a stroll. Eligia saw a mango tree, went closer and saw some ripe mangos hanging from a lower branch. She couldn't catch the mangos from the ground. The branch was a bit higher for her height, out of her reach to grab the mangos. So, she went up climbing the tree. The branch from where the mangos were hanging was fairly horizontal and safe to climb. She was fine while climbing but as soon as she tried to grab one of the mangoes with one hand while keeping her balance with the other hand, she suddenly slipped from the branch supporting her and fell on the ground. Fortunately, the grass on the ground cushioned her feet but still she suffered some light sprain in one of the ankles. She said that it was paining. So, we decided to get back to Mérida as soon as possible.

Once we got back, the very first thing we did was to head straight to our apartment in a hurry! Fortunately, the elevator was working, and she didn't have to walk up the stairs. Once we reached our apartment, we asked her to relax on the living room sofa. I had some Vick's, and with that I gave a good massage on her ankle for a while. After ten minutes of rubbing the ankle, the pain was totally gone. It was probably a very light sprain from impact, but she was impressed by my first aiding! Then we had some coffee prepared by our expert barista, Bolivar. Thereafter, we drove them to Laddy's place.

After knowing Laddy's parents and siblings well, we used to visit them regularly and they used to come to our place. Laddy and Bolivar started dating frequently. I had my regular classes plus building a new lab. I couldn't go out with Eligia that frequently. Sometimes we two used to go to a movie, but not that frequently. One day in our apartment she showed me how to concentrate mentally. We two sat down not too close to each other, fairly well apart putting a blanket on both of our laps and each one concentrated on a particular theme or scenery, individually without consulting with the other. After ten minutes, we would face each other and relate our experience of concentration. After many years when I started Yoga lessons, I realized that she was teaching me a technique of meditation.

We four used to go out on a double date on the weekends. During the weekdays I had very little time for amusements. I was teaching new courses in a new language, fixing lab experiments plus writing technical papers for presentation in national and international conferences. Next year in 1975 I presented papers in England, USA, Brazil and also at an Interamerican Congress in Caracas. I also got involved with IVIC (*Instituto Venezolano de Investigaciones Científicas*). 1974 – 75 was a very busy year for establishing myself academically in Venezuela. It was the time when due to the oil embargo and manyfold price rise of gasoline, Venezuela was booming with its petrodollar income, and I was interested in establishing myself in Venezuela. Attracted by petrodollars people came to Venezuela from many other countries of Asia, Europe, and America, both from North and South. Two Indian professors, Dr. Prakash Chand, and Dr. Maharaj Singh Tomar joined our Physics Department. Prakash came with his wife Mahima and two little kids, Bandana and Ajay.

Maharaj came alone but after a while his girlfriend from Bolivia joined him. Dr. Michel Mouton came all the way from a rich country like Switzerland. Michel came with his young family, wife and two little sons.

After a while Maharaj, Michel, Roberto, and myself became very good friends. We used to spend our spare time in a small bar near Plaza Bolivar close to the campus. I still remember crystal clear that one fine morning in a weekend I heard a knock at the door of my rented house; I opened the door and there was Maharaj with a beautiful blonde by his side. He smiled holding her hand and said, "Here is Ana, my girlfriend as I told you earlier. She arrived from La Paz only yesterday." From that day on Ana became a family friend for us. She saw our kids born and growing up in Venezuela and afterwards in Canada. Likewise, we saw their family flourishing in Venezuela and the USA.

Eligia lived mostly with the family of Doña Juana, although she had a rented room with her friends in *Edificio La Vencedora*, another apartment building like our building *Mis Muchachos*. I used to visit her more often at Doña Juana's family, and eventually became a good family friend. Doña Juana had three little kids: Domingo Negrita and Cheo. Eligia was very fond of them, and *vice versa*. There were times when Doña Juana would invite me to have afternoon coffee with them. Those were the times when I would feel absolutely free to mingle with them. Doña Juana would cut local jokes and Eligia would wink at me to understand those humors!

Bolivar and Laddy were going strong with their love affair. Nevertheless, my friend was not happy with his teaching job. He was looking for something better and suddenly moved to Caracas where the opportunities were much better with higher salaries. I was a bit disappointed, but they kept in touch with each other through frequent phone calls. As Bolivar moved out, I felt the apartment was too empty for me to live alone. I moved to a small house a bit far from the university, but my brand-new Hillman was very trustworthy in reaching the campus early in the morning. Eligia moved in with me after a few months of seeing Jay suffering in loneliness.

The rented house was in a very good neighborhood. It was right beside a small police post, good for security. On the other side there was a little store where we could buy things for daily households, mainly food, drinks and stationery. The owner was a young, friendly gentleman. We called him *Señor* Pascual. People around were simple and friendly. Within walking distance there was a big park and a discotheque for entertainment in the evening. We used to walk in the park in the evening and then to the discotheque casually for a cold drink, generally a beer.

My little Hillman was very handy for traveling anywhere. Once we went to see the family of one of Eligia's friends, Nelly. After crossing the mountainous area, driving up to the topmost point *El Pico Bolivar* (that I remembered passing by when coming from Caracas for the first time!) and then descending to the plains of Valera where Nelly's family lived. People in this part of Venezuela are very simple and friendly. I met Nelly's mother and grandmother for the first time, but they treated me as if they knew me for years! There I ate a big *arepa* filled with cheese, my favorite food, and a large coffee. Once we finished eating, Eligia got up and signaled me: *Let's get back!* I was surprised. Driving three hours to reach here and only in half an hour of staying to hit the same road back again! But anyway, when you are in love, you are prepared to do almost anything for your beloved! Driving back the same track was nothing, I pondered. We reached home late in the evening. Next day was a Sunday, no rush to get up early!

As the Christmas holidays approached, we decided to take a longer trip all the way to the north-eastern tip of Venezuela along its northern coastal highway. The highways on the plains of Venezuela were splendid, three lanes on each side and very well maintained. Leaving very early at sunrise, we passed Valencia, Caracas and hit the eastern region. In Puerto La Cruz, a tourist town, we stopped for a late lunch in a beachside restaurant. They specialize in fresh fish caught right there. We, of course, both ordered fish, and the waiter asked what kind of wine we'd like. Then he added, "We have good white wine to go with fish." I was very ignorant about wines (even after living in Germany for three years!) and asked him: What will happen if I drink red wine with my dish of fish? He enjoyed my innocent inquiry and replied: "Oh, nothing will happen, no stomachache!" We all laughed aloud at his joke.

Then we continued driving to Carúpano, almost near the northeastern tip of Venezuela, and stayed there overnight in a small hotel. Next morning, we went to the seashore and collected a lot of seashells. Taking a dip in that crystal-clear, saffron colored water was extremely freshening, heavenly! After checking out, we drove to the extreme end from where you could see the coastline of the island of Trinidad. This reminded me of the other British colonies in the Caribbean basin: Jamaica, Guiana, and several other smaller ones. We had a typical lunch, again on the beachside. It was goat meat with spicy rice. I never had goat meat since leaving India. I was very excited about this goat meat recipe. The waiter was an elderly, knowledgeable person. He could explain to me the history of goatmeat in that area of Venezuela. During the early period of British colonies, many people of Indian origin who lived in Trinidad and Tobago, simply moved to the eastern part of Venezuela. They brought their culture, and hence their culinary art, with them. The waiter's explanation was convincing. He added that many Venezuelan families in that region had Indian last names coming from their ancestry.

On the way back we stayed one more night in Carúpano. Again, we took an early morning bath in the crystal-clear Caribbean Sea, ate lunch with fresh fish, spicy rice with white wine and headed back to Caracas, and then to Valencia where Eligia's family lived. They lived in a small township called *Naguanagua* right on the outskirts of Valencia, the big industrial town after Caracas in that region. It was late afternoon when we reached Naguanagua. As we parked the car in front of the house, her mother and some brothers and sisters came out to receive us. It was an ambience full of hugs and kisses among the siblings and the mother. Then Eligia introduced me to her family, and we all relaxed in their family room. Her mother, Doña Ignacia, quickly went to the store next door, and Gina the store owner helped her to quickly get some packets of flour for making *arepas* and, of course, fresh cheese, *queso guayanés*. She went straight to the kitchen and started *creating* the big arepas. In an hour we all had a great dinner with arepas filled with cheese, a hot broth of black beans and white rice. It was very filling and fulfilling!

After dinner we went up the spiral stairs at the other edge of the big living room, with the small luggage with very limited items we carried, and her mother showed me the room for me to stay. Eligia would sleep with her two sisters in the adjacent room. The second floor had several rooms to accommodate all the siblings of Eligia. The brothers were Chui, Pepe, José, Luingo, Chama, Rafael and Eligio. Luingo was adopted when he was a baby, of the same age a José. The rest were all blood brothers. Eligia had two sisters, Milagros and Lucía. It was a big family in a limited living space but without much problem. This again reminded me of the families in India with so many people living together in small quarters that became more intense when the refugees from East Bengal arrived in Calcutta/Kolkata. The same thing is happening right now in the southeastern part of Bangladesh with refugees from Burma/ Myanmar. This is now the biggest refugee camp in the world supported by the United Nations.

Next day we went to *Las Trincheras*, an area of tourist attraction for its natural thermal-mineral bath, very well organized with pools at different temperatures as well as a "mud-bath" with minerals, very good for arthritis and other rheumatic pains. We took with us a few siblings of Eligia in my little Hillman. Each day we stayed there we would take them in turn so that everyone had a chance to get the mineral water bath. Chui, brother next to Eligia, became very friendly with me and that friendship continued for many years to come till we moved to Canada. I found him to be a very simple and sincere person, and we talked about many things of broader interest worldwide rather than only the local gossip.

After the Christmas and New Year holidays we drove back to Mérida, starting from Naguanagua very early in the morning. Nevertheless, it was a long drive with only two stops: a short lunch break in Acarígua and a still shorter coffee pause in Guanaré, before climbing the serpentine mountainous and narrow "highway" to Pico Bolivar and then gliding down to Mérida. We reached Mérida quite late in the evening!

Next morning, we were both ready to go to work! Eligia and I used to make weekend trips to nearby places, sometimes longer drives even to *Pamplona* in Colombia, passing by *Cúcuta* and *Pamplonita*. In Pamplona we made good friendship with an Arab merchant who had a store in the town, and he used to give us small gifts every now and then. We also went to the other adjacent parts of Colombia, such as *La Guajira*, passing through the dry areas of *Machiques* in Zulia bordering Colombia. Venezuela had excellent highways and we never had any problems while driving. Once we took a longer trip to *Asunción,* the capital of Guajira and then traced back to *Rio Hacha*, continuing all the way to *Santa Marta*. That was the farthest point we drove in Colombia.

It had been quite a few years since I left home in India in early 1962, now over twelve years. During those past years I had made true and sincere friendships with many people, lived with excellent families worldwide, but really didn't have a family life of my own. So, I decided to approach Eligia to marry me for I was now eager to have the experience of growing my own family. At first, she was a bit surprised, perhaps felt a bit uncomfortable at such a straight forward approach. She responded pensively, saying, *"Piénselo bien!"* (Think it over!). But later she agreed!

We made a trip to the nice little town of San Lázaro to get her Birth Certificate. We drove through the most colorful town of Boconó, which became famous when Simon Bolivar passed through that town. When his army was marching through the main street of Boconó, the ladies of the town crowded on the balconies on both sides of the road to greet *El Libertador*. He looked up at the ladies to receive their greetings and in return responded bowing down to the ladies,

"*¡El Jardín de Venezuela!*" From then on, Boconó was called the Garden of Venezuela!

We stayed in a small hotel that had no shower in the bathroom, but a tank made of cement and filled with water. You had to use a big mug to take water out of it and pour the water with your hand on your head. I told her that we had the same bathing system in our home in Calcutta. On her first visit to India, she remembered that and reminded me. The paperwork for her new birth certificate was ready the next day. I also had no birth certificate and had to do it in Mérida. They needed two witnesses for certifying my date of birth, although the place and the date of birth were in my passport. My friend Roberto and his wife Zófia became my witnesses for not having my birth certificate and they also had to testify that I was single, not already married elsewhere. Roberto joked: I don't trust the Indians like you. Maybe you already have a Harem in Calcutta!

Our registration for the marriage certificate was very simple. There was no ceremony at all. It was a working day. We went to the registration office with two witnesses again. This time Doña Juana was her witness, and my witness was the baker who had his shop on the ground floor of the same building where I lived. After signing the papers, Doña Juana embraced Eligia and uttered, "*Oh, mi flaca!*" (Oh, my slender girl!") and the baker Luis gave me a tight hug, "*¡Felicitaciones!*" ("Congratulations!"). Then they departed and we both went back to our work, she to her hospital duty and I went straight to my department to give lectures. In the evening, two of us celebrated privately with a candle-lit dinner in a restaurant, *La Casa Vieja* (The Old House). That was our most favorite hangout place in downtown Mérida near the university President's office.

Next morning, I broke the news to my boss, Professor Néstor Joussef. He gave me also a big hug and said jokingly, "Welcome to the club of the sufferers!" Then I went to my office that I shared with Dr. Roberto Suárez. Roberto was genuinely happy to hear the news and said, "So, Jay, finally you are settled with a Latin American after going around the world!" Both Joussef and Roberto spread the news to other colleagues, and they all came crowding our small office to congratulate me. Miguel Rada was also very happy, because he was the first faculty member to receive me in my small hotel room when I landed in Merida only a year and half ago. Once I decided to create my own family, things went fast. Thanks to Eligia!

Eligia and I had a simple and quiet life. We both enjoyed travelling, making short trips to the nearby places like Lagunillas, Tovar, Bailadores and many other small towns. The area around Mérida was very picturesque. Mérida was also a place of tourist's attraction because of its famous *Teleferico* (ropeway), longest and highest in Latin America. It had five stations, the last one was at El Pico Bolivar, over five thousand feet high. Once we went to Bailadores to attend the wedding ceremony of Professor Joussef's sister-in-law and then continued our trip to Colombia, staying overnight there in a small hotel in Cúcuta. We still have a picture of that place, Eligia sleeping and maybe dreaming, and I with my afro-hair, a bit hippie style in front of our room.

Our first son arrived in July 1975. We named him *Kumar*. A week before his birth, Doña Ignacia came from Valencia to help us. She was an expert with experience of having so many kids of her own. When I mentioned this to her, she joked, "But I didn't work like a midwife for delivering them! There were others to help me out." When Eligia's labor pain started Doña Ignacia and I nursed her a little bit and then we three (four!) drove to the University Hospital where Eligia friends and coworkers, Laddy and Sonia were working in evening shift that night. What a good coincidence! Everyone in the hospital knew Eligia, and it was like a family affair in the University Hospital. Dr. Avendaño, the physician on duty who was supposed to deliver the baby, was also known to Eligia. So, Doña Ignacia and I felt very relaxed and came back home without any anxiety. Next morning the phone rang and Sonia's voice on the other end was full of delight, "Jay, it's a boy! The baby and the mother are in good health. Come whenever you can. No hurry!"

Doña Ignacia made a small breakfast for both of us and took something for Eligia in a small packet. It was a really cold morning, I remember. Doña Ignacia and I waited in front of the entrance of the hospital till the visiting hours started at 8 AM. While waiting I got some hot coffee from a small cafeteria in front of the gate. We both drank the freshly brewed delicious coffee to get rid of the cold wind blowing on our faces. Once the visiting hours started at 8 AM, we went up to the third floor and entered the room where Eligia was still sleeping. We didn't want to wake her up and went to the next floor to see the baby. It was a large glass covered area full of cribs, each one with the baby's name (or the parent's last name) on. A nurse helped us to find Kumar's crib, for Sonia had already left after finishing her night shift. We saw Kumar moving his head as if waking up from a good night's sleep. It was quite an excitement to see my own son! Doña Ignacia embraced me in delight and a few joyful teardrops rolled down her cheek. This was after all the birth of her first grandson too!

We went back to Eligia's room. She was having her breakfast. We told her that the baby was fine and looked good. She smiled showing signs of relaxation at the news, and

Doña Ignacia gave her a soft kiss on the cheek. I felt great at that moment seeing the mother and the daughter in unison. After a while we left so that Eligia could have some more rest. Doña Ignacia and I did some shopping for the newborn and the mother. Doña Ignacia was an expert in that area while I was totally ignorant. She packed a few items that Eligia might need for the baby and for herself, and we came back to the hospital in the evening. I didn't bring flowers. That was a mistake! But I brought a thin book, a Spanish translation of Tagore's *Geetanjali*! It was a collection of about twenty plus short poems (like Pablo Neruda's *Veinte Poemas de Amor y Una Canción Desesperada*). But that little book of poems fetched Tagore a Nobel Prize in literature in 1913! Eligia was happy to get a different type of gift for celebration, not a bunch of red roses! Then a nurse came in with the crib and handed the baby in the mother's arms. Another moment of delight I couldn't express in words. Doña Ignacia bent over to see the baby. Eligia looked deep into the baby's twinkling eyes. A new chapter in her life had just started! And a new chapter in my life as well: A Family Life!

1975, the year my first child *(Primogenito* in Spanish) Kumar was born, was one of my best years, academically and professionally. I went to England to present one of my research papers at the International MTDR (Machine Tools Design and Research) conference. In the same year I presented other research papers in Rio, Brazil and in Caracas, Venezuela. Right after getting back from Caracas, Kumar was born. In fact, some of my colleagues in Caracas were kidding and joking with me," What are you doing here, Jay? You should be beside your wife now!"

Doña Ignacia stayed with us another week. In the meantime, we found an elderly lady to help Eligia in house spousing and with the baby. Venezuela's maternity leave was very good, nine months! That helped to keep the newborn in mother's arms in the budding months of life. It was also less anxiety for a mother to take care of the baby firsthand. I also started coming back home as early as I could after finishing my duties at the university. Roberto, my officemate, and a great friend used to tease me.," Aha, Jay, now you are leaving earlier for the baby! How about the mother of the baby?"

That was a great time in my personal development having a baby in the family. I learned a lot about taking care of a newborn, like feeding, cleaning, putting to sleep, etc. When Eligia started working I used to be more careful with the baby Kumar. Then she became pregnant again, only a few months after coming out of maternity leave. I thought that it was a great strategy of Eligia to continue several intermittent and prolonged maternity leaves in a row, and eventually we could end up with a dozen kids, a full soccer team and a referee! She commented with her usual smile, "It needs two to make a baby!"

A girl was born on November 2, 1976. We were both very happy to have a pair! We already selected a name for a girl: *Anyana*! The word '*Anjana*' in Sanskrit has several meanings. Since *j* in the Sanskrit language (and in English!) is pronounced as an *y* in Spanish, so for the sake of a "correct" pronunciation we changed that *j* in the original Sanskrit word '*Anjana*' to *y* in our modified '*Anyana*'. At that time, Venezuela was flooding in Petrodollars, and I didn't think of leaving Latin America back to Canada or Europe. I thought that this slight modification in spelling, from *Anjana* to *Anyana*, was acceptable. Probably in later years our daughter had to explain to her schoolmates, college friends and working colleagues in Canada and USA that she was not just another 'Any Ana' but

Anyana in Spanish pronunciation, or *Anjana*, as pronounced in Sanskrit, the mother of all Indo-European languages! Probably she will need to give the same explanation to her colleagues. Recently, she asked me about the meaning of her name, and I gave her some good illustrations from Sanskrit literature. I think that *the Buddha*'s daughter was named *Anjana!*

With two babies and two of us with full-time jobs, our life took a busy turn. Eligia tried to get night shifts in her hospital duties so that I could work during the day and take care of the two infants at night. It was not an easy job for her! I was also not very good at taking care of newborn babies. It was a new learning process. I still remember that I used to keep Anyana in the crib, keeping it as close to the bed as I could, and keeping Kumar on the bed itself with me. I had to be very careful about not 'squeezing" him with my body weight!

By the end of 1976 I got a very good job offer from a new "National and Experimental" university in San Cristóbal, a nearby city that we passed through so many times while driving to Pamplona in Colombia during our earlier happiest, hippiest years.

I had to inform the university authorities about my future move. Professor Joussef was disappointed at my resignation, but we stayed as good friends till today. Roberto was a bit sad since we were such good colleagues in our shared office and great family friends outside the office as well. Doña Juana was also a bit down as her *'mi flaca'* would be leaving Mérida soon. Eligia's other friends, especially Laddy and Nelly, had similar feelings. I told them that the good part was that they would have another place to visit, San Cristóbal and, of course, the country fair of San Sebastián!

By mid-January, after the year ending festivities in Mérida were over, we moved to San Cristóbal. The moving was quite adventurous. We hired a small truck with the driver, and he drove in front of our little Hillman with a few household belongings, beds, kitchen table, chairs, sofa sets, etc. we had collected over the last two years. It was a trip of over three hours with Eligia beside me and Anyana on her lap and Kumar in the crib strapped in the back seat. Not a comfortable journey but we enjoyed it, stopping at the same cafeteria in El Vigia, where we shared coffee and *pasteles* for the first time three years ago. At that time we were four traveling together: Eligia, Laddy, my friend Bolivar and me (plus the taxi driver). This time we were also four: Eligia, me and our two babies: Kumar and Anyana!

Since I couldn't find any rented apartment nor a small house in San Cristobal, I arranged temporarily for our "sheltering roof" in Rubio, a small nearby town, about an hour's drive from the university campus in San Cristóbal. It was simply a very large room with a small kitchen and a bathroom. It was previously rented as a store, not a comfortable dwelling for the four of us. While I was at the university, Eligia was all alone all day in a new place without knowing anyone, and especially with two infants. She was very anxious and told me once that it felt like living in a prison cell with two kids. Fortunately, a colleague, Professor Horacio Rey, found for us a nice three-bedroom apartment in a new building, *La Bermeja*, in San Cristóbal, not too far from the university campus. It was a great help from Horacio, and we maintain our friendship even today through long distance phone calls and "virtual visual contacts" by Facetiming with smartphones, thanks to WhatsApp!

Eligia felt much better at this new move. The building had a huge park across the road and a hospital, *Policlínica de Táchira*, right in front of it. Many faculty members lived in the same building with their families. Eventually, we made friends with several families. There was Professor Amancio Rodríguez and his wife Aurita with their two young children, Jaime and Graciela. They were from Spain and lived in Brazil before coming to Venezuela. Through Eligia and Aurita, we became very good family friends. There was another Chilean family of Professor Rubén Priess, his wife and one son. Rubén's parents were originally from Germany but moved to the USA after the Second World War and lived in New York. When they came to visit Rubén, I had a chance to meet them and practice my German after so many years. We felt something in common, living in several countries over many years.

In the 1970s in Chile, after the fall of the socialist president Salvador Allende and the government taken over by the military dictator Augusto Pinochet, many well-educated Chileans migrated to Venezuela and got positions at several universities. Both at ULA in Mérida and at UNET in San Cristóbal, many Chilean educators with excellent academic preparation contributed to teaching, research and in restructuring the academic programs and revising the syllabi of many courses in the Faculties of Engineering, Science, Arts and Business Administration. At ULA, I came to know Professor Suárez and Professor Miranda in Chemical Engineering. At UNET, I worked with many Chilean colleagues within and outside our Faculty of Physical Sciences that included Engineering. Professor Maruja Al Ruiz, her husband Jaime and daughter Daniela became our family friends. Daniela was of the same age as Anyana. They all came several times to our house in Las Vegas de Táriba.

One such visit was to celebrate the birthday of Anyana, and Daniela had a great time with Anyana, and all the other neighborhood kids invited for the birthday occasion.

Our Department Head at UNET was Dr. Valerio Wong, a Chinese Venezuelan, born in the Petropolis of Maracaibo. He did his Doctorate at the University of Birmingham in England. There he met many Indians and formed close friendships with some of them. One of them was Dr. Mihir Das. Later, after many years of living in Venezuela, I met Dr. Das. He came as a Visiting Professor in Maracaibo, and Dr. Wong invited him to UNET for lectures. I met Dr. Das for the first time at UNET, and again in Kolkata, India and in Mayagüez, Puerto Rico.

Our youngest son Nayan was born while we were still living in La Bermeja, and *Policiínica de Táchira* was right in front of our building just across the road. It was so easy for Eligia this time! When her labor pain started, she just walked with me to the clinic, registered herself and walked up two floors instead of taking the elevator. When I asked, she explained to me that she walked because the birth of the baby would be easier and faster, good for the baby and for her. Then she threw her usual smile. She was right! Nayan arrived within a couple of hours. A normal birth without any complications for the mother as well as for the baby. I was waiting in our apartment and once the phone rang to give me the good news, I just crossed the road to the clinic, went up two floors and saw Nayan in the big room where all the newborns were in their cribs waiting to be taken care of. The nurse took me to Nayan's crib. The baby blinked his eyes, perhaps to say *hi* to his dad. I remember there was a lot of Johnson's baby talc powder on his face. I had to sign a paper and the nurse accompanied me with the baby to Eligia's room.

I took the baby out of the crib and put him on Eligia's arm. Her eyes flashed in delight!

That week I finished a summer laboratory course with only a few students, about five or six. I invited them for food and drink in a nearby restaurant called *El Platanál*, which specialized in typical local dishes, basically with plantain. I also invited a few of my Colombian friends: Horacio Rey, Jaime Salcedo, Rafael Serrano and Julio Pava. Doña Ignacia went with me to the clinic and Lucia, her youngest daughter stayed home to take care of Kumar and Anyana. She was very happy to see both Eligia and the baby *Nayan* in good health. On the way back from the clinic, we bought some gourmet food for Doña Ignacia, Lucia, and some baby food for Kumar and Anyana. They were still babies when Nayan was born. Hence the baby food.

Then I drove to El Platanál to celebrate with my students and friends. It was a two-way celebration party; one for Nayan's arrival and the second for finishing the summer course in time. When I reached the restaurant, they were all waiting for me. Upon seeing me entering the pub room they all stood up and clapped in unison! Then they all hugged me one by one, both the colleagues and the students, and uttered with big smiles: ¡*Mucha Felicidad!*

I felt so relaxed that evening while I truly enjoyed being with my colleagues and students with good food and beer. We spent a couple of hours there talking about our school, soccer games and many other topics including Venezuelan as well as international politics. The food that accompanied our conversations was delicious and spicy with a plantain-based gourmet. Hence the name of the restaurant was *Platanál*, meaning an area of plantain trees. When we finished eating and drinking, they all wished me again the very best for the baby, Eligia and the whole family. The waiter was also very happy with a generous tip. Besides, I asked the waiter to pack some good food for Doña Ignacia and Lucia. They both were surprised when I entered the apartment with a big packet of gourmet smelling food. Lucia loved it.

Now that we had three infants, we thought of moving to a house rather than living in an apartment. Through one of our secretaries, Benilde, I met a very interesting person who was building small houses. He built Benilde's house too. Mr. Jacob was originally from the German speaking side of Switzerland but also lived in USA. He didn't like USA and moved to Venezuela. He was an engineer by profession. Upon arrival in Venezuela, he first lived near Caracas, built a few small houses there in the touristic beach areas, made good money there and then moved to *Las Vegas de Táriba*, a quiet area only about fifteen to twenty minutes' drive from our university. Benilde took me to him, a tall and slim man but with a robust personality. Benilde might have already talked to him about me and my plans for a house. He was very glad when I personally told him about my wishes to live in a house with my small and growing family. He showed me a plot adjacent to his own house. The location was very good, right near the entrance of the area. I could see some other small houses around the area under construction. I felt it was a safe area for our growing children, since there would be neighbors coming soon once those other houses were fully constructed. So, I agreed.

Eventually, Mr. Jacob showed me a floor plan he had already made. It was more like a bungalow with its living room, kitchen and three bedrooms in the front entrance; behind this part a small patio and on the other side of the patio three smaller rooms. The house would be surrounded by a small plot for gardening and there would also be a covered garage for one car. I liked his plan, especially the small plot around the house, since in the apartment there was no such luxury of nature and Eligia used to do her "gardening" in small tubs and put them to decorate our apartment's balcony. That open area would be also good for chilling with our family friends with a few beers and snacks at the weekends.

Mr. Jacob and I sat together and estimated the costs of the land, materials for construction, labor plus his profit. We were both engineers, and so there were no secrets from either side. The total came out to be 400,000 Bolivars (Bs), the Venezuelan currency, that was roughly 93,000USD. He asked for 100,000 Bs as down payment and the rest I could pay in installments. I found it to be a good deal and agreed. Mr. Jacob put his four sons to hard work, and the house was complete in six months. We moved to our new home leaving a string of loving memories and nostalgia for the apartment building where we made friends with so many families, especially Amancio and Aurita as well as Rubén Preiss.

It was quite a different feeling in a house than in an apartment. Our three little infants could play around on the natural ground rather than on an apartment floor. Eligia also had much more space for gardening. On our apartment's balcony, she had the only option to plant in the pots. She spent all day at home with the three toddlers while I was having a variety of entertainment at the university. Thus, the open-air gardening kept her healthy, and more importantly, happy. Slowly we started making friends with our immediate neighbors. Eventually, Eligia made a strong bond of friendship with one neighborhood lady. *Doña Flor* and her husband were originally from Colombia, but they migrated to this part of Venezuela, almost bordering with Colombia, when they were very young. All their children were born in Venezuela; and there were many. Eligia became a very good friend of Doña flor and some of her elder daughters: Beatriz, Marta and Sandra. She had two sons: Pedro and Giovani. Pedro was a big soccer player and Giovani was a very bright student in his class. Doña Flor's husband was a quiet person. We could hardly see him.

In the meantime, I made a good friendship with Mr. Jacob. He used to invite me in his open-air balcony for drinking beer and talking in German. I was the only person around with whom he could speak in his own native tongue. Mr. Jacob used to smoke cigar while drinking beer and I used to enjoy joining him in smoking a cigar every now and then. We mainly conversed on his old time in his native Switzerland, and I maintained our conversation talking about my three years of training in Germany. Since he was originally from Switzerland, the neighbors used to refer him as *El Suizo*. El Suizo was a very active person, always supervising his three elder sons, Jacobo, Isaias and Isaac, in the construction work of small houses.

Some of our university friends used to visit us in our new home. Maruja and Jaime, natives of Chile, used to visit us with their daughter Daniela who was of Anyana's age. In one of Anyana's birthday parties, many kids from the neighboring families came, including the younger children of Doña Flor plus Daniela and the daughter of another Mexican lady. So, we had an international family here just like in the apartment building, La Bermeja. Eligia had more space here in the open air for gardening and house spousing with three toddlers than within the four walls of an apartment. Initially, I used to spend my spare hours with Mr. Jacob, drinking, smoking cigars and practicing my German. Later, I became a member of the local Rotary Club and started getting more involved with the Rotarians. Through the Rotary Club, I met other professionals like medical doctors, lawyers, and businesspersons. This association with Rotary in my life continued till today and gave me the chance to get involved in several service activities and had the opportunity to experience the convention of the Rotary International in Atlanta, USA and Toronto, Canada. Currently I am a Paul Harris Fellow in Rotary International.

As Kumar, Anyana and Nayan reached their Kindergarten age, we found a good school in San Cristóbal. A new routine in our daily life has started. I started taking them to school on my way to the university, and Eligia started feeling lonely in the house. My little Hillman was full of three toddlers, and I started practicing English with them, mainly singing a few songs I knew. One of them, I still remember, was a very famous American song: *Oh, you are a wonderful baby, a wonderful child; I found a million-Dollar baby in a ten-cents store.*

My job at the university was as usual, but I presented a few papers in the national and international congresses during those years and got promoted to Full Professorship in 1979. Some of my research work in manufacturing processes and systems was in the same line of work of a Japanese professor, Dr. Takeshi Kurimoto, who was working at the Universidad del Oriente, in Puerto La Cruz, Venezuela. He liked my work and sent a strong recommendation letter to our university authorities and that also helped me to get the promotion. During 1980 -82, I presented a few more papers at the ASME (American Society of Mechanical Engineers) conferences in San Francisco, California. One was the Centennial celebration of ASME, and the conference was on Advances in Materials Technology in the Americas. The other one was a Tribology conference on Wear of Materials. In this second conference, I took Eligia with me, and as always Doña Ignacia took care of our kids. She was always very helpful and responded positively with much delight.

In San Francisco, Eligia and I stayed in a small hotel right in front of Sheraton where the conference took place. It was the time when Venezuela was still booming in petroleum exportation while the oil price went up worldwide. We went out to do some shopping for the kids. At one shop, knowing that we were from Venezuela, a salesgirl remarked jokingly, but not sarcastically, "Please bring us a can of gas on your next visit!" I still remember the joke. In 1983, the oil demand changed drastically, and suddenly the very stable Venezuelan currency over many decades, dropped from 4.30 Bs per US Dollar to some 7 Bs./Dollar. I could sense this decline to go on and decided to move my family back to Canada. After applying to several places in Ontario, I got a positive reply from Queen's University at Kingston offering me a Visiting Professor's position in its Mechanical Engineering Department. I immediately accepted the offer and started preparing for another move, this time with a family with three little kids. Kumar was not yet 8.

I talked with my department Chair, Rafael Serrano, and he understood my point perfectly. My main point was that the future education of my children was very important for our family. My other Colombian friends, Horacio and Jaime, were positive minded to my situation. My Venezuelan colleagues understood my point, especially Amancio who was always a good colleague and a great friend throughout my six and a half years of work at the Universidad Nacional Experimental de Tachira (UNET). The Dean of Research Dr. Ramírez Martínez, a great scholar and educator, was always helpful and agreeable with my situations. He suggested: Jay, why don't you take a Sabbatical Leave for a full year and see how the current conditions in Canada are. I thought it to be great advice for not resigning and disconnecting totally from UNET. Thus, I applied for a one-year Sabbatical Leave with full salary. The condition was that if I would continue staying in Canada after the Sabbatical, I should return the money of the 12 months' salary. I found it quite reasonable and agreed.

Kumar, Anyana and Nayan already had their Canadian ID cards with pictures, because I presented them to the Canadian Embassy in Caracas after they were born. This time I applied at the Embassy for their Canadian passports and got them without any problem. For Eligia's Permanent Resident's visa on her Venezuelan passport, we all had to travel to Caracas, a long ride from San Cristóbal. We stayed in a hotel near the Canadian Embassy. Next morning, we had an appointment at the embassy. The lady who interviewed Eligia, was very happy to see our Canadian "family" with three little Canadian kids born in Venezuela. She stamped the Resident's visa on Eligia's passport without any question. Within half an hour Eligia got her visa to stay in Canada as long as she would like!

On our way back we stayed a couple of days in Valencia with Doña Ignacia to celebrate. Everyone was very glad that Eligia got her visa without any hassle, but there was a mixed feeling of happiness and nostalgia on Doña Ignacia's face. This would be the first time that her first child would be leaving Venezuela, and she wouldn't be able to see her that often. Eligia's two sisters, Milagros and Lucia were also a bit sad since they used to come sometimes to us in San Cristóbal. Lucia came and stayed with us for a while when Nayan was born. That was a great help to Eligia since Kumar and Anyana were still infants. Milagros also stayed with us for a while at one time. I still remember that we all went to Rubio, a small town where there was a lady fortune-teller who could see the future. My friend and colleague Dr. Jorge Müller came with us. He was very interested in his future even at his advanced age!

We slowly started packing the necessary items and giving the rest to our friends and families who needed some of them. Eligia had a very small TV that could be easily carried with us. Eligia had it since her college years, but we gave it to Rigoberto, a technician, and a colleague of mine, who really wanted it. Eligia didn't oppose it! Similarly, we had to get rid of many items that we used over the years and eventually had developed sentimental values for them.

Before we left, Maharaj and Ana María came from Caracas to stay a few days with us before saying goodbye. Doña Juana came from Mérida with her three children Mingo, La Negra and Cheo, and we had a great time over the weekend. I remember that we went to see the movie *Gandhi* in a drive-in theater and then to an ice-cream stand. Many other local friends came to say goodbye and "*hasta pronto*" to us. It was always a mixed feeling of departure that I went through so many times since leaving India, but it was a new transition for Eligia. This was the first time she would be leaving her own country, her family and friends for a longer time! I could feel her feelings!

Now that the official part of the move, such as the visa for Eligia, Sabbatical Leave for me, were all done, I started to work on finding our living quarters in Kingston, Ontario in Canada. Luckily, I got a two-bedroom apartment of the university residence facilities where most of the visiting faculty, students with families stay. Besides, the paperwork with the university and with the Mechanical Engineering Department was properly done before we had to leave. Then we bought our tickets to Toronto, Canada with a few days of in-between stay with our friends Imam and Evie in New York. In July 1983 we set sail for Canada after the usual goodbye hugs and teardrops from all our loving friends and families in Venezuela.

BACK TO NORTH AMERICA

It was a bright afternoon when we landed at Kennedy Airport. Imam and Evie were at the airport as always. This time the kids were a bit bigger and Nayan was not sick, not like the last time when we arrived from India. We all hugged and kissed. They were so happy to see our kids a bit grown up now. Evie raised Nayan in her arms and Imam held the hands of Kumar and Anyana, and we walked to the parking lot with Eligia and I carrying our small luggage items. We brought just the necessary things to start a new life.

    The next few days in NYC were full of joy. Imam and Evie took the kids to so many places, now that they were almost 8, 6 and 5, and could appreciate new places and things. We went to many museums, art galleries and a Canadian circus, *Mon Soleil* (My Sun) that was going on in New York. I still remember that Evie took a picture of Kumar, Anyana and Nayan sitting in front of the big entrance gate of the Museum of Natural History! Then the circus-show of Mon Soleil in a huge tent full of people was exciting for the kids. That was the first time they were watching a live show with tigers, lions, elephants, monkeys, and even colorful peacocks on a stage!

    One week with Imam and Evie went flying as always good times go so fast! They took us to the city's local airport La Guardia for a shorter flight of about an hour to Toronto.

Again, the same goodbye hugs, but no teardrops. It was a joyful *adios* hoping to unite as a family again once we could get settled in Kingston. At Toronto International Airport, we were warmly treated by the immigration officer. He was happy to see little Canadian kids with us returning home, and after signing the papers, he said with a big smile: Welcome home! We were also very excited at this heartfelt welcome and hired a taxi all the way to Kingston for only 120 Canadian Dollars! We reached Kingston in less than two hours. We headed straight to the *An Clachen* university residence area and inquired to find that our apartment was ready. We got the keys from the office and were all set to enter our new home! Both the taxi driver and me were very happy.

It was a two-bedroom apartment fairly roomy and most importantly, it was on the ground floor, especially thinking about the safety of the kids. Once the taxi driver left, we unloaded and arranged a few things that we brought with us from Venezuela. Then we moved around the block to get a feeling of the area and found a small restaurant at the edge of our residential area just across the road. We all five of us entered and sat at a table near the window. Kumar, Anyana and Nayan were all excited to discover a new eating place in a new country!

There was a big shopping mall right across the road from An Clachen, our residential complex. After our breakfast we entered the mall and bought some of the essential items to start a new living experience in a new country. The beds, mattresses, kitchenette table and four chairs and any other heavier items were all delivered free to our apartment. That was a pleasant surprise not common in Venezuela. Once all the essential items were delivered, Eligia and I started arranging them in the living room and in the bedrooms while the kids went out to play in the green area right outside our apartment. This way a ground floor apartment was very convenient for the kids to get out in the open space as well as for their safety. The weather in June – July was lovely in Kingston with nice and warm sunshine throughout the long daylight time. For our evening meal, Eligia did some small cooking, experimenting with the stove, fridge and our brand-new utensils. After eating we all sat around the small TV we just bought and entertained ourselves with the Canadian channels. The kids enjoyed the cartoons even though they didn't know much English. It was a longish day, and we were tired from traveling, shopping, and getting adjusted to a totally new environment. We went to bed early.

The next morning the first thing we did after breakfast was taking the kids for admission in Centennial School that I arranged through correspondence from Venezuela, knowing the education of our children as one of the most essential items of our move to Canada. The school was within a couple of blocks, about five minutes' walk from our residence. As we entered the small, one storied school building, in a row of five newcomers one following the other, and presented ourselves in the main office, a gentleman in his fifties came out of the office and introduced himself to us as Mr. Davidson, the Principal of the primary school. He shook hands with Eligia and me and hugged the kids with a smile and said to them: Welcome to Micky's hut in the Disney World! They all giggled for they remembered Micky from the comics!

The paperwork for the admission procedure was very simple, short and straight forward since the school already had the necessary information about our children that I sent from Venezuela. After finishing that part as we were almost coming out of the office, again in a line of five, Mr. Davidson suggested to leave the kids with him in the school so that they could get around and get acquainted with other kids of their respective classes. He hugged them again and held their hands. As we were leaving them with Mr. Davidson, Kumar and Anyana looked at us pensively and a few teardrops rolled down Nayan's cheek! He was only five and a half and thus was admitted in kindergarten.

We walked back to our apartment – our new home – and worked for an hour or so to finish the touches that were left to be done the night before. Eligia looked happier this morning after a goodnight's rest and from seeing that the admission for the children in Centennial School went through smoothly. That was a great relief for both of us! It was almost the lunch hour, and we had a small lunch by warming up the leftover from last night. Eligia kept working after lunch and I packed up a few papers in the briefcase that I needed to present for starting my work in the Mechanical Engineering Department at Queen's University. McLaughlin Hall, the main building of the Mechanical Engineering Department, was also close to our residence, only about ten minutes' leisurely walk. It was a pleasure to walk that distance in a beautiful summer afternoon.

Most of the buildings at Queen's were of a relatively older architectural design with strong and thick columns, in a style like those at Princeton and Harvard in USA. On reaching McLaughlin Hall after a nice and slow walk from An Clachen, I headed to the main ME office and introduced myself to the girl at the desk. She seemed to recognize my name and after a smiling 'hello' took me to the office of Professor Norman Kirk, who was the Department Chair at that time. Professor Kirk, a short structured man like me and in his mid-fifties, shook hands warmly and asked me to sit down in front of his large table. After a few introductory information about the ME Department, he stood up and asked me to follow him along the narrow hallway. Near the end of the passage, he stopped in front of a closed door. I looked up and was very surprised to see my full name, Jayanta Banerjee, on the nameplate at the door. He smiled at my happily surprised face and opened the door with a key he already had in his pocket. We got into the room. It was a fairly large room, lightly furnished with a desk, a couple of chairs, bookcase, a small blackboard, a noticeboard and a coat hangers rack. The most attractive part of this private office of mine was the wide wall to wall window that overlooked the beautiful scenery of the pine trees under the blue backdrop of a beautiful summer afternoon. Professor Kirk handed me a pair of keys, one for the room and the other for the main entrance of the building and whispered with a smile: keep them carefully.

Then he took me to different offices to introduce me to some of the faculty members. It was summer vacation and only a few were present. Finally, he took me to Professor Rice's office. As he knocked on the door, a tall and slim gentleman probably in his early seventies, opened it and Professor Kirk introduced me to him: Here is Dr. Banerjee with us! Professor Rice looked genuinely happy to meet me as his smiling face and a very warm handshake suggested. He said "Professor Banerjee, welcome home! Here in Kingston, you are not too far from Waterloo, your Alma Mater." It was a good feeling to receive such nice welcoming words from Professor Bill Rice, since I was supposed to work with him during my one-year tenure as a Visiting Professor at Queen's.

Professor Kirk left me with Professor Rice and went away. Before leaving us, he assured me that he had already done the formal paperwork for me but needed me in his office to sign a few forms after I was through with Professor Rice. After Norman Kirk left, Bill Rice and I sat leisurely, and he mentioned that he was glad that I got back to Canada with some cross-cultural experience in Latin America. He talked about his own Sabbatical leave experience at MIT, working with Professor Nathan Cook, his old friend over many years. He also mentioned the work of Professor Rabinowitz who worked with Professor Cook on the problems of Tribology (meaning problems of friction and wear in mechanical systems). He even mentioned the name of my Waterloo boss, Marc Hillier, and his own academic association with Hillier. Thus, talking with Professor Rice, gave me the confidence as if I am coming back to my own academic and professional family in Canada and it was receiving me with a welcoming hug. I felt happy at the very onset of my tenure at Queen's.

After describing his own Sabbatical experience at MIT, Professor Rice asked me how my experience in Latin America contributed to my professional career and personal education. I summed up my experiences in Colombia for almost three years with CUSO (Canadian University Services Overseas) and then in Venezuela for 10 years where I formed my family. He was very glad to hear about my cross-cultural experience in Latin America. Later, he used to visit us in our humble apartment and play with our kids and enjoy Venezuelan coffee freshly brewed by Eligia. Professor Rice was a perfect gentleman, born and raised in Montreal, and equally fluent in English and French as his native tongue.

As our joint "teaching assignment", Professor Rice and I started offering a course on Manufacturing Processes twice a week. He would elaborate on the theories of a manufacturing system, and I added the experimental work and my own industrial experience as "evidence" in support of his theories.

We worked together for two semesters offering the same course. While working with him, I did some research on "Rolling of Flat Plates", similar to what my friend Pablo Barreto conducted at Waterloo. Professor Rice helped me a lot based on his own lifelong experience of research in manufacturing processes and especially lent me his own desktop computer for working! He brought it personally to my office and in that way, I could work privately in my office without going to the common computer room for the faculty and graduate students. I am ever grateful to Professor Bill Rice for his kindness! Besides, his visits to our family were a true pleasure. Our kids, at that time 8, 7 and 5 years old, loved to play with him, and he used to enjoy drinking freshly brewed Venezuelan coffee prepared by Eligia.

During that year I wrote a couple of papers on Rolling and published them in a refereed journal of ASME (American Society of Mechanical Engineers). I wanted to put Professor Rice's name as my co-author, but he said that just putting his name in the acknowledgement section at the end of the paper would be good enough. I agreed to his suggestion and acknowledged him in both the papers for his help and encouragement in my research. I will never forget his enthusiasm and help in my work, and more importantly his humbleness in visiting our family and sharing a joyful time with our kids.

At the end of one year, my Sabbatical assignment in the Mechanical Engineering Department at Queen's was culminated, but I didn't want to bring my family back to Venezuela, nor did I want to live in Venezuela alone without my family. So, I negotiated with the university in San Cristóbal (UNET) and returned the university my one year's Sabbatical salary. It was a happy win-win solution for both.

Professor Rice was so kind that he sent me to the University of Winnipeg to his friend Dr. Ostap Havaleska, Chair of ME Department so that I could get a faculty position there. But I didn't get the job. In the meantime, Eligia started studying for an associate degree in fine arts. The entire program was for three years. Thus, I was unemployed with a family of three little children while my wife started as a fulltime student. Fortunately, I had some money saved over years of working. So, I decided to become a fulltime student myself. This time I thought of getting a master's degree in Education and got admitted easily in its program for already possessing a doctorate degree although in a different field: Engineering. Our entire family became a *student family*, with Eligia and me in higher education and the three children in primary school!

In the Faculty of Education at Queen's, Professor David Pratt became my advisor for the M.Ed. program in which I was registered. Professor Pratt worked with Benjamin Bloom (famous for Bloom's Taxonomy!) before coming to Canada. I finished all the required courses during the first year of my study and only the thesis work was pending. So, I started looking for a full-time job and got one at the University of Vermont (UVM) in Burlington, USA. I needed money to support my family and couldn't stay eternally as a graduate student. My position at UVM was Associate Professor in the Department of Mechanical Engineering. Professor Clarke Hermance, the Chair of the ME Department, was extraordinarily nice with me. He arranged for my teaching duties only from Tuesdays to Thursdays, three days a week, so that I could commute to Kingston on Thursdays in the late afternoon and get back to Burlington on Mondays in the evening. This arrangement helped me to stay with my family three days a week and do my M.Ed. thesis work at Queen's plus maintain a full-time job at UVM!

Eventually, David and I became good friends. We used to exchange residence over the long weekends. There were weekends when I'd stay with my family in Kingston, and David would travel with his son to Burlington, stay in my apartment and they would go skiing on the famous slopes of Vermont. This arrangement worked well over the long winter months. I used to drive every weekend from Burlington to Kingston and back through Montreal, some five hundred miles back and forth. The border guards at the check posts between the USA and Canada became so familiar with my face, seeing me twice every weekend, that they would allow me to drive through without opening and checking the trunk of my little Chevette.

In Summer 1986, Eligia completed her Fine Arts degree, and I finished all the requirements for an M.Ed., and we were ready for another move, this time from Kingston, Canada to Burlington, USA. Our good family friend Gurnam, (my buddy at Waterloo!), came all the way from Moncton, New Brunswick to help us in moving. We hired a small truck from Hertz's Rent-A-Car, fitted all our material belongings in it, bid farewell to our loving neighbors at An Clachen and drove away leaving the city of Kingston behind and keeping the treasure of its four years of memories in our hearts. I drove a truck for the first time in my life, and Gurnam followed me with the Chevette and my family.

In Essex Junction, not very far from Burlington, we rented an apartment, like the one we had in Kingston, only a bit bigger, now that the kids were four years older since we left Venezuela. The children's school was also in Essex Junction, and the school bus used to pick them up right from our doorsteps every morning and bring them back in the late afternoon. This time they got used to a bus ride rather than walking to school. Eligia became a fulltime house-spouse again after completing her degree in Fine Arts. I got used to commuting between Essex Junction and Burlington's UVM campus, passing by another small town named Winooski. It used to take about forty-five minutes each way.

My work at UVM was much like that at Queen's, teaching manufacturing processes and conducting some research. However, this time I became more interested in engineering education rather than in the hardcore of mechanical engineering only. At the ASEE (American Society for Engineering Education) Annual Convention in Reno, Nevada I organized a full session on implementing courses of humanities and social sciences in mechanical engineering program. Two of my UVM colleagues, Dr. Jeff Leible, and Dr. Jean-Guy Belliveau joined me in that seminar. However, due to my lack in research output, I didn't get tenured. Rather than extending my contract year by year, I decided to leave UVM and, hence, had to look for another job.

During my three years of work at UVM, I made many friends. There was a math professor from Spain, Dr. José María Gambi, who came from Valladolid accompanied by his wife and three children, just like us. Soon we became very good family friends, and Eligia could once again socialize in "real" Spanish, her native tongue! Since leaving Venezuela, she was mainly in an English-speaking environment in Kingston, including her Fine Arts classes, but she kept conversational Spanish with the kids at home. This way our children never lost touch with Spanish. They are still fluent in their Spanish they learned from their mother and practiced with her throughout their adolescent years and now in adulthood. I reflected again in the German proverb, "*Übung macht den Meister*" which is very true, especially in learning any language!

There was another interesting personality at UVM with whom we got befriended within a short time. He was Professor Branimir von Turkovich, a professor in Mechanical Engineering. We used to call him by his nickname: *Branie*. Branie was originally from Belgrade, Serbia, a part of ex-Yugoslavia, but lived in many countries including Spain, before embarking in USA. His wife, Doña María, was from Spain. Thus, we had another Spanish connection among our family friends! Branie and Doña María came a few times to our place. He used to enjoy spicy chicken curry of East-Indian style prepared by me. They also invited us a couple of times to their home on special occasions like celebrating their marriage anniversary. His passion was roasting a full pig. Our youngest son, Nayan, got scared watching a 'real' animal getting roasted and rotated on fire!

Apart from Branie and the Gambis, Jean-Guy also became a good family friend. He invited us a couple of times to his place. As a good French Canadian from Québec, he was a great wine lover, and I combined it with real hot-spicy Indian curry, making a good gourmet combination. Another young faculty member came from Princeton. He was originally from India, of Bengali origin, and I had the chance now and then to practice my native tongue with him.

This way three years at UVM passed smoothly without any major adventurous event but I needed a more stable job. I started looking for a faculty position in mechanical engineering or in an allied field, and finally found one in Puerto Rico, another Spanish speaking country within the commonwealth of USA. Nevertheless, we wanted to keep continuing the education of our children in English medium.

Also, Eligia liked more the quiet and peaceful environment of Canada. We decided to move our family back to Canada again! While in Kingston, we made strong friendly bonds with a Venezuelan couple, Yolanda and Francisco (Frank) and their children: Berna, Doris, Frank and Francis. They moved to Ottawa around the time we moved to Vermont. They bought a house in Gatineau, just across Ottawa river, in the French sector in the province of Québec. But it was only a stone's throw from downtown Ottawa, only ten to fifteen minutes' drive. Thinking about our children's higher education in future and the proximity of Ottawa, Canada's capital, we decided to buy a house in Gatineau.

Francisco and Yolanda helped us a lot in selecting the house. Eligia and I had to make a couple of trips to finally purchase a small two-storied house in Gatineau. Even though Gatineau was in Québec, there was an English Middle School where we enrolled Kumar, Anyana and Nayan. Frank and Francis, Yolanda's two younger ones, were in the same school. By then, Berna and Doris, the elder daughters of Yolanda, were already at the University of Ottawa. With so many moves, from Venezuela to Canada, from Kingston to Essex Junction, two moves within Essex Junction, and now back to Canada, our children (and we too as a family) got much used to adjusting ourselves to a new environment and always with good spirit, good vibes!

This time, *Chiquito*, our little pet – a crossbreed of German shepherd and something else (?) – whom we got in Essex Junction as a new member of our family - moved with us. Chiquito had to get the shots and the vaccine certificate like any pet, for crossing the USA-Canada border and migrate to a new country, just like us. Again, this time our friend Gurnam Singh came all the way from Moncton for helping us to move back to Canada. Two moves with a family between Canada and USA within three years was not easy. But we did it with a sportsman's spirit and with joyful disposition to know the unknown.

In Gatineau, the school for the kids was of English medium for the main classes but there were French language courses as well. Kumar had the advantage in French because he was in half English and half French immersion in his classes in Kingston. I still remember my conversations with Mr. Davidson, the Principal of the Centennial School in Kingston. When I put Kumar in English with French immersion, he got very concerned. He told me," But Dr. Banerjee, Kumar's home language is Spanish and school language is English. Now, another French immersion! Will it not be too much for a little kid?" I smiled and replied politely, "No. I have seen in Colombia and Venezuela little kids speaking several languages fluently. In Cali, Colombia, a friend of mine was German and his wife, French. They put their son in an English medium school, and the street language in Colombia is Spanish. And the boy spoke four languages fluently. Similarly, I saw in Venezuela a little girl, named Amrita, speaking Bengali, Spanish and English equally well. She talked with her parents and with me in Bengali; with my wife in Spanish and with her parents' American friends in English!" Principal Davidson nodded his head with concern. After four years, when we left Kingston, he agreed: "Dr. Banerjee, you were right when you put Kumar in English-French immersion!"

As I mentioned before, when I was almost leaving UVM, I got an offer from the University of Puerto Rico in its Mayagüez campus, where I applied for a position in its Mechanical Engineering (ME) Department. Dr. Fernando Plá, the Chairperson of the ME Department called me on the phone, and we started our conversation in English. When he came to know that I worked before in Colombia and Venezuela, he asked me in Spanish, "Can we switch over our conversation to Spanish?" Probably he wanted to see how good my verbal Spanish was. I immediately switched over to Spanish and we continued the rest of our conversation in Spanish. And he offered me the position of a Full Professor right on the phone! To me it looked like that Dr. Plá was more impressed with my verbal Spanish than my academic transcripts. Since I had no other job offer in Canada or in the US, I accepted his offer half-heartedly. It was not an easy decision for me to leave my family in Canada just after settling down in Gatineau. The only positive point of assurance was Yolanda and Francisco living right beside us. I was sanguine that they would help Eligia with anything she would need and especially at any emergency.

In one sense I was relaxed knowing that Gatineau was a safe place very close to Ottawa, the capital of Canada, with all the facilities of a modern living in a peaceful environment including the scope of higher education for Kumar, Anyana and Nayan. Eligia also felt more secured and stable in Canada than in USA. The presence of Yolanda and Francisco as a friend and neighbor was an added support. Besides, I talked with the school's Principal and gave him my phone number for consulting with me for any suggestion at any time. This way I felt much better emotionally before leaving for another new challenge in Puerto Rico.

On August 10, 1989, I left for Puerto Rico with a short couple of days halt in Vermont to sign some papers related to the closing ceremony of selling our house in Essex Junction. That was the last thing I needed to do in Essex Junction, and I was glad that I could sell the house finally, and it helped me with the down payment on the house we purchased in Gatineau. Apart from signing the closing documents, I could see some of my colleagues and friends in Burlington, mainly at UVM. Professor Hermance was happy to see me again and we recollected during our brief conversation our old connection at Waterloo. In 1965, when I started as a graduate student at Waterloo, he joined our ME Department as a young faculty after finishing his PhD at Princeton and a Post-doc in Sweden. His wife was Swedish. His lab was adjacent to our manufacturing lab and one of his PhD students was my good friend, Nat (Natarajan). I came to know Professor Hermance through my buddy, Nat!

Next morning, I took a flight to San Juan, Puerto Rico with a short stopover in New York. In San Juan, I had to take another very short flight in a 12-seater small propeller plane to Mayagüez, situated at the western end of this small island. Professor Plá, a tall and handsome man in his early fifties, was at Mayagüez airport with his little daughter about eight or nine years old. After a warm handshake and some initial whereabouts, he took me to a hotel – Hotel La Palma – and on our way showed me a bakery store and cafeteria called *El Ricomini*, and suggested that next day, a Sunday, I could enjoy a good breakfast there, for the other restaurants would be closed on a Sunday. That was a good tip which I follow even today after some thirty-three years, because El Recomini has the best coffee and the freshest sandwiches in the town.

The hotel room was small but very clean. I was a bit tired of traveling with two stopovers at JKF and San Juan. I went to bed early. Next morning, a Sunday morning, was a bright day, and the Caribbean sunshine was flooding the city. After having a good breakfast of a cheese and egg sandwich plus a 12 oz coffee at El Ricomini (as suggested very strongly by

Dr. Plá!), I took a long walk of two hours, since I had nothing else to do till the next day, a Monday, and I didn't know anybody either to pay a visit. The downtown has the central plaza – *La Plaza Colón* – with the cathedral at one side and the municipal hall on the opposite side in a typical Spanish colonial style. This is a typical structural order almost all over in Latin America, and Puerto Rico is no exception even with all its modern US influence. I also took a tour within the university campus where I would be starting to work the next morning. Who knew for how many years! The campus was in a flat area not too far from the hotel. It was deep green all over the campus with a host of mango trees along the roads within the campus. From the sign on each building, I could find the general library, the post office within the campus, the Students Council office, the cafeteria, and finally the Mechanical Engineering building (where I would be reporting to Dr. Plá next morning!).

On the next morning - a bright Monday morning - I reported to Dr. Plá in his office. It was a busy day, the first day of the Fall semester. Despite his very busy schedule, Dr. Plá introduced me to several colleagues, and then showed me my office and handed me over a set of keys, one for the office and the other for the entrance of the faculty area on the second floor. His own private study-room, apart from the Chairperson's general office, was right in front of my office across the hallway. My office was a nice room with the wide window overlooking the skyline of Mayagüez and the steps going down to one of the five entrances of the campus.

Slowly, I started organizing myself and my office with a few books and teaching materials I brought with me. I was scheduled to instruct a few sections of a manufacturing teaching lab. The supervisor of that lab was Dr. Rodolfo

Lithgow, a very senior faculty member of our department. In fact, Dr. Plá and a few other senior faculty members were his ex-students. Dr. Lithgow, originally from Dominican Republic, did his undergraduate at this university and then did his PhD at Texas A & M. So, everything was a small family here with Dr. Lithgow, Dr. Plá and their senior colleagues.

As a new faculty member, I started getting acquainted with my colleagues. There were two other instructors recruited in the same year of 1989 in January. They were Dr. Paul Sundaram and Dr. Néstor Pérez. Paul was from India and Néstor from Venezuela. Our department had a good international flavor with Dr. Ali Sabzevari from Iran, Dr. Arshad Khan from Pakistan, and Dr. Mohan Muju from India (who joined at the same time with me as a Visiting Professor). Dr. Muju and I were in the areas of manufacturing processes and systems, and both started offering a course on Manufacturing Processes. Eventually we became very good friends and started traveling together. He bought a small, secondhand car, a Mitsubishi Mirage, and I became his driver! We enjoyed the weekends driving around this tiny and beautiful island. The Puerto Rican call it *La Isla del Encanto*, meaning the Island of Enchantment.

I also became a good friend of Dr. Ali Sabzevari. He was a very well-traveled person. He was also in India recruiting good professionals for his hometown university at Shiraz when he was in Iran and had a high position at the University of Shiraz. We both lived at the university residence, an apartment building named Darlington Building, mainly occupied temporarily by the foreign faculty members and the student athletes. It was a twelve storied building. The two top floors were reserved for the student athletes and the rest of the building was occupied by the professors and the graduate students with families. Professor Sabzavari and I were single, lonely souls, since both of our families were living abroad, his in USA and mine in Canada. So, we used to go sometimes in the late afternoons after our classes were over, to a nearby *Colmado*, a small grocery store where you could hang around with a few cold beers accompanied with some sizzling-hot and delicious typically Puerto Rican snacks like *empanadillas* and talk about our world trotting experience. I enjoyed listening to his anecdotes in the Asian and European countries, and I used to tell him about my stories in several Latin American countries I worked. We both used to enjoy the relaxed atmosphere, just standing outside the entrance of a *colmado*, and sharing each other's memories while sipping some cold beers and munching hot, typically local snacks of spiced cuts. This helped us getting over the nostalgia of living away from our families with growing adolescent children.

Another Indian faculty member in our department was Dr. Nellore Venkataraman, with whom I got quickly befriended, probably because of our similar age and for our work experience in other South American countries. He did his PhD at Purdue, and then went to ISRO (Indian Space Research Organization) and worked with Dr. Abdul Kalam (Ex-President of India who was also a physicist!). Nellore came to Brazil around the same time I went from Canada to Colombia in the early seventies. *Venka*, as we used to call him, had a very rewarding experience in Brazil, both professionally and culturally. He worked at a Brazilian Space Research Center near Sao Paulo. He liked Brazil very much, especially the friendliness of its people with the foreign workers. He used to tell me many stories about his good neighbors in Brazil. The very day he arrived in Brazil with his young family, his wife and a toddler daughter, the next-door neighbor lady came to his house with a pot of coffee and some snacks to greet them. He and his wife, Nirmala, knew no Portuguese and the neighbor lady knew no English or Tamil! Such was his first Brazilian experience of fellow feeling! Both Nellore and Nirmala enjoyed Brazil. He left Brazil for its economic instability in the 1980s, the same reason I left Venezuela. I left Venezuela and brought my young family to Canada. Looking back now that was the best decision I had made at that time for my family. My children, now grown up and well established professionally, agree with me.

At UPRM I had several good friends: Nellore, Ali, Néstor, and a few other younger faculty members. Often on Friday afternoons, Dr. Plá and Professor Ken Soderstrom, another senior faculty who was the department Chairperson before Plá, would join us at a *colmado,* a standing pub, very close to our ME building *Lucchetti.* We used to drink a few cold beers and gossip about the talk of the town and about our university. Other than that, we used to have occasional lunch together, including the faculty, the administrative staff and grad students. Our building had a big, open-air terrace on the second floor, and we used to get together for our "potluck lunch", each one bringing some food or drink. Although drinking alcohol on campus was prohibited in theory, Dr. Plá allowed it on such special occasions. Even the Rector used to join us to sip some good wine! On occasions, I cooked some spicy Indian Chicken Curry and Dr. Benítez, another senior faculty of Plá's contemporary, gave me ride to bring the big pot of curry and rice from my apartment! I didn't have a car in the beginning.

During the first few years, I used to go back to Canada as many times as I could, at least during Christmas, Easter and in summer vacations. It was a wonderful feeling each year to see our children growing, passing from intermediate school to high school and eventually getting admitted at the University of Ottawa. Eligia was single handedly spearheading everything from grocery shopping and cooking to taking care of the adolescent children, at a time when smoking pot and consuming other harder drugs were so common in high schools. She gave an outstanding performance during those years in Gatineau, and I am ever grateful to her for her resilience and patience in bringing up our children through those years.

During those summers, I used to take advantage of the engineering conferences in Toronto and Montreal, presenting and publishing several papers at CSME (Canadian Society of Mechanical Engineers), similar to ASME (American Society of Mechanical Engineers). It was also an opportunity to meet my good old friends from Waterloo. Eligia accompanied me once to Toronto and once to Montreal. What a pleasant surprise it was to suddenly meet my Waterloo colleague Tom Shankar at a CSME convention in Montreal! During the first ten years in Puerto Rico, I was quite active in research, presenting our results at different conferences and publishing them in refereed journals. Unfortunately, I didn't have the same blessings for fetching research grants from different federal agencies, like NSF, NIH, etc. Professor Néstor Perez and I wrote three proposals on materials for manufacturing. But they didn't fly, and I stopped writing proposals. Instead, I started concentrating on Engineering Education, and eventually became a Life Member of the American Society for Engineering Education (ASEE) where I was a Professional Member since 1971. I wrote several short articles on my experience in teaching engineering since 1965, when I was a TA at Waterloo. Some of these articles were published in the section *Last Word,* in *Prism,* a magazine of ASEE. Others were presented in several local conferences in Puerto Rico as well as in the ASEE annual conventions in the USA. I felt happier working with ASEE in its mission of improving engineering education and teaching in general, rather than researching a very specific technical problem in manufacturing engineering.

In January 1999, I had a minor heart attack, not a massive one, and a stainless-steel stent was implanted in my heart. During that time, a lady at our university, who was working then at the office of Graduate Studies, took very good care of my health. My stent implant procedure was conducted in San Juan because we didn't have those facilities here in Mayagüez at that time. An ambulance took me to the University Hospital in San Juan, and after a few days, Dr. David Serrano, a great humanitarian, and an ME faculty colleague brought me back to Mayagüez. Upon returning to Mayagüez, during the recovering period, the lady at the Graduate Studies office again took very good care of me. David Serrano took me to her house, and I stayed there for a few weeks before going back to my apartment in Darlington Building. It was during those weeks I was very much impressed by her unselfish friendliness, service, and compassion for me. Eventually, I got emotionally attached to her unconditional friendship!

Our friendship became closer and deeper as months passed by and in one short vacation, we took a weeklong boat trip on one of the Caribbean cruises very common in Puerto Rico and in the other Caribbean Islands. The cruise ship touched several smaller islands like Martinique, St. Lucia, Guadalupe, etc. and returned to San Juan through Santo Domingo, the capital of Dominican Republic. It was a wonderful one-week holiday on the Caribbean Sea with a lot of entertainment during the day at each port, and music and dance on board in the evening. The trip was so exciting and at the same time relaxing, that we two repeated similar short trips together. One of them was at Puerto Plata, a great beach resort on the northern coast of Dominican Republic. I was much impressed by the hospitality in Santo Domingo. We used to organize technical conferences in Santo Domingo for its proximity from other Caribbean and Central American countries, and furthermore it was a great tourist attraction at a much less hotel costs than in Puerto Rico.

Eventually, I had to tell Eligia about this affair of mine with the lady at Graduate Studies. Also, I didn't want my grown-up children to accuse me: Dad, you are cheating our mother! So, in October 2000, Eligia and I had a peaceful divorce. She didn't even have to come here to the court in Mayagüez. My lawyer and a good friend, Carlos Vargas wrote the Divorce Decree, sent it to Eligia, and she simply had to sign it and mail it back to my lawyer. My daughter Anyana, then a professional with a Master of Public Health degree and working at the Center for Disease Control and Prevention in Atlanta, (after finishing her Graduate Studies at Emory), was a bit upset but finally understood me and agreed with this quiet settlement between her mother and I.

Now that I was officially divorced, I could tell you the name of that fine lady in the office of Grad. Studies. She was Matilde Muñiz Troche, a Puerto Rican, born and raised in Mayagüez. All her family members, closer and distant ones, were *mayagüezanos*, and she felt very proud of her ancestors. Everyone called her by her nickname *Matty*, and she was known all over in her extended family and friends' circle as well as at work by that nickname! She used to invite me to her family get togethers. There I met her brother and three sisters, and many cousins, nephews and nieces and their children as well as grandchildren. It was a huge extended family just like in India! I felt very comfortable in such a family environment and its warmth that I remembered from my childhood and adolescent years in India, many decades ago! Because of this cultural similarity and affinity within the extended family members, I got much attached with Matty's wider family circle in a surprisingly short time. In a ceremony of *qunceñera* (like the *sweet sixteen* celebration in USA and Canada!) of one of her nieces' daughters, I met all her distant relatives and their families.

Puerto Ricans, in general, are family oriented. It is a small island, and within fifty miles of your home, you have someone of your relatives, your distant family. I learned this family trend while studying Cultural Anthropology under Professor Allan Philbrick at the University of Western Ontario during 1972 – 73, before moving to Venezuela, and after returning from Colombia. He used to call it *Central Place Theory*. According to this theory, if you have your "extended" family within a commuting distance from your home, you don't need other social connections. While I do respect a lot of Professor Philbrick's ideas, I don't quite agree with this theory. Even in a small community you can have your "joint family" connections as well as friends from the neighborhood outside your biological family, like in India!

My work at the university was usually offering two courses a semester, one at the Graduate level and the other Undergraduate, mainly in the areas of Mechanical Design and Manufacturing Processes & Systems. In the first few years I was assigned for the lab courses as well. This way I got to know all the lab technicians of our ME department and became very friendly with them. In the later years, I was assigned only lecture courses. Apart from regular teaching, I tried to fetch some funds for improving our Manufacturing Processes lab and got one for buying equipment. With that money, we bought a set of experimental equipment mounted on four wheels for teaching Materials Forming to the undergraduates.

In 1995, we organized here the First World Congress on Intelligent Manufacturing Processes & Systems. Professor Vladimir Milacic, a Visiting Professor from the University of Belgrade in Serbia, spearheaded the initiative for organizing this international conference, and scholars from all over the world attended. Professor Birendra Sahay, another Visiting Faculty from the Indian Institute of Technology (IIT) at Kanpur, India, worked side by side with Professor Milacic in crowning this conference with great success. Delegates came from many Asian, European and, of course, from the American continents, and that made the social component of a technical event full of joyful interactions. Professor Nam Suh, the ME Chair at MIT, came as a keynote speaker. Similarly, other eminent engineering scholars came from Holland, Germany, England, and from several other European countries, and, of course, from Serbia, the home country of Professor Milacic.

Professor Milacic stayed here as a Visiting Faculty for three years. Eventually, we became family friends. He came with his wife, *Dragna*. Dragna and Matty became very good friends, and the four of us often went out together in the weekend evenings for dinner and dance. Dragna and Matty were both very sociable and outgoing personality and got along very well. In many sunny afternoons, we two happy middle-aged couples would go out for lunch on a pristine Caribbean beach in Rincón, only a fifteen minutes' drive from Mayagüez, and enjoy lunch with a few drinks. Professor

Birendra Sahay joined us a couple of times. He came alone from India. We didn't want him to feel lonely on the weekends. Moreover, Birendra was my friend at Waterloo. We both did our Doctorate there and we have lovely memories as students in Canada and as young faculty members at IIT, Kanpur in India. After so many years thereafter, getting together again in Puerto Rico was an extra plus!

The Second World Congress on Intelligent Manufacturing was celebrated in Budapest, Hungary. I was able to attend it. It was again a great pleasure to meet Vladimir and Dragna there. Because of proximity between Belgrade and Budapest, Vladimir and Dragna came by train. Train journey in Europe is a pleasure, like in Canada. Besides delivering conference lectures, most of the time we spent in sight-seeing and enjoying good food plus the superb wine of Hungary. Because of my Bengali taste for hot and spicy curry, I loved Hungarian *Gulash* and ate it almost in every meal during my stay in Budapest. There were also so many historical and architectural marvels to visit in that twin city of *Buda* and *Pest*, hence, the combining name, Budapest. It was a full week of delight. I still remember clearly that I took Vlada and Dragna to the train station on their way back to Belgrade, and then on the same day I took my flight back to San Juan.

During my second Sabbatical leave from the University of Puerto Rico in 2005 - 2006, I spent most of my time at the University of South Florida (USF), working with a young Indian professor, Ashok Kumar. He was very helpful and arranged some financial support for one of my graduate students, Boris to work in his lab for a few months. He also had many graduate students of Asian origin, mainly from India and China, and he used to take very good care of them. Ashok invited me several time in his home for Indian dinner plus watching Hindi movies on TV with his family. It was a very inviting environment every time I visited his family.

There was a Japanese Post-doc, Dr. Makoto Hirai, working in Ashok's lab. We shared the same office, became good friend, and even practiced some conversational Japanese that I learned from a course I took at UPRM. I had a small car, and Makoto and I used to make short trips in the weekends to the nearby tourist spots, like St. Petersburg, St. Augustin, Miami Beach, etc. Makoto taught me how to select a really good *Sushi* and also how to eat cold soup. He was very hardworking, a typically dedicated researcher. One morning I arrived earlier than usual in the lab, and to my surprise, I saw Makoto already working there! I uttered aloud, "Makoto, you came even earlier than me!" He responded with a humble smile, "Dr. Banerjee, I didn't go home last night." My God, he worked all night! Makoto was very much devoted to his experimental research with Physical and Chemical Vapor Deposition (PVD and CVD) of nanoparticles! He wrote several papers within a very short period and published them in the referred journals. He even put my name in the acknowledgements, simply because I edited his English.

I was trying to wet my feet in *Nano-Tribology*, meaning friction, wear and lubrication in the range of nano scale. Dr. Ashok Kumar had a couple of graduate students, one Indian and one Chinese, who were working in the same field. I worked with them on the experimental side and got some papers published with the results I got while working with them. Both helped me a lot. Later, the Indian student named *Raghu* got a good job in California, and we stayed in touch for several years. The Dean of Engineering at USF was Dr. Louis Martin Vega, and the Chairperson of the Industrial Engineering Department was José Zayas Castro. They were both from Puerto Rico and worked at UPRM as faculty members. Once Louis invited me for lunch and we enjoyed ourselves in a local Tex-Mex restaurant, recollecting our old time in Mayagüez. We had occasional coffee breaks with José. I went a couple of times to Gainesville to see my good friends there whom I came to know on my first visit to the University of Florida (UF) in 1985 when I was working in Canada. My professor George Tlusty was gone by now, but I could meet some younger faculty members like Professor Yogi Goswami and several others.

After returning from the Sabbatical leave, I changed a bit my focus and tried to work again on the general field of engineering education. I could publish a couple of one-page articles in Prism, the ASEE magazine, and then a book, *Third Side of the Coin,* and published it in Penguin Pocket Book series. Around those years, I wrote a few more books, in total nine, five in English and four in Spanish, and could publish them through a subsidiary of Penguin, called *Palibrio* in Bloomington, Indiana. They publish both in English and Spanish. In one of the books, titled *At the Crossroads of Emotion and Reason*, I tried to summarize my views on engineering education as it was practiced during 1980 – 2000. Dr. Robert Sherwin, a professor of English at the University of Puerto Rico, was kind enough to write the introduction.

This time my family life started in a different domain, with Matty and her family, her children, grandchildren, cousins, nephews and nieces, and other distant relatives. Puerto Ricans, just like our East Indians, keep good ties with their distant relatives, the way our societies started after the great agricultural revolution. While getting more involved with Matty's family, I kept myself in close contact with my own children living in Canada and USA. I also tried to maintain a formal and friendly relationship with their mother, Eligia.

Matty and I started traveling in many countries, first within the nearby Latin American Caribbean culture, plus Mexico and Central America. We liked Mexico so much that we went there many times, almost once a year. My son, Kumar joined us with his young family a couple of times on the beautiful beaches of Puerto Vallarta on the Pacific coast of Mexico. Then we expanded our travel domain and went to Argentina, then a longer trip to Europe, and finally all the way to India. We both love traveling, meeting new people and making friends in different countries and in diverse cultures. This is more interesting than studying them from books!

In Argentina we had a great time in Buenos Aires, Bariloche and the Iguasú Falls. In Buenos Aires the public transportation was excellent. We spent there a full week without taking a taxi and went to many places even on the outskirts of the city limit. One Sunday morning we took a bus to a country fare, *La feria de los Mataderos* and met so many people from outside Buenos Aires! We came across a group who came all the way from Mendoza, a city closer to Chile. I found them very open-minded and jolly-good people, drinking and dancing throughout the entire morning and continuing up until the late afternoon. I remembered that Dr. Plá's wife, Doña Gloria, came from Mendoza. There were many shopping plazas we visited in Buenos Aires. One of them was *Plaza de San Telmo*, famous for its antique collections, including out-of-print books, posters, souvenirs, and a lot of ceramic pottery.

We were lucky to get a hotel room near the famous Cinco de Mayo central plaza of Buenos Aires. We walked to the main railway station, close to the presidential palace. I remember one day there was a workers' strike (quite common in Argentina and throughout Latin America!) and the road to the presidential palace was blocked by the police, and we couldn't walk to the railway station. During our stay in Buenos Aires, we mostly walked in the downtown districts without any problem. The downtown restaurants were always full of people, and the food was great, both in quality and quantity, and much less expensive than in USA and Canada. I used to drink alcoholic beverages those days, and both of us enjoyed a glass of wine with our meals every day. Wine was served in big glasses, as big as beer mugs.

We flew from Buenos Aires to Bariloche. The most impressive sight was the lake *Naguel Whapi* in the middle of the city, crystal clean and serene, reminding me of the Amerindians worshiping their Serpent god *Naguel,* or the Tibetan monks meditating on the lake *Manasarovar* in the Himalayas We had some interesting experience at a bar in Bariloche. We were taught how to dance *tango.* A young couple came and asked us to dance with them. We switched partners, Matty dancing with a young man and I with a young girl. They showed us all the steps to fit and follow tango music, and we practiced with them several songs. Then they came and sat with us at the same table. We talked and listened over hours, accompanied with good Argentinian wine, of course, and some snacks. Our warm conversation with this young couple, added with red wine and warm snacks, was memorable. We realized that they had a tango teaching club. Then an elderly person joined our table. He introduced himself as a professor of tango dances. Later, he described his experience in other countries teaching tango. He even went all the way to Japan for teaching tango in Tokyo!

We returned to Buenos Aires and the very next day took another flight to *Iguasú* Falls. We were lucky to find a hotel not too far from the falls. We walked to the falls following a long, narrow, and winding path. Once we reached in front of the falls, Wow, what a majestic view! Iguasú is a series of eleven falls, crystal clear waterfalls falling parallelly one beside the other. It was a very different panorama, comparing with our Niagara Falls between Canada and USA. The Iguasú Falls is also shared by Argentina and Brazil for hydroelectric power and, of course, for tourism. Niagara Falls has a better view from the Canadian side. That is why most of the tourists from the US side cross to the Canadian side for watching it. Especially on a moonlit night, the reflation of moonlight on the turbulent water falling straight into the gorge almost vertically is simply a hypnotic beauty. The eleven falls of Iguasú have a beautifully harmonious symmetry!

Here in Iguasú, people cross to the Brazilian side to view the falls. We were much eager to go to the Brazilian side to watch it. It was a once in a lifetime chance! I had no problem with my Canadian passport. Canadians needed no visa to enter Brazil. But Matty with her US passport needed a tourist visa. We were so interested to see the falls from the Brazilian side that we inquired about where to get the required visa just stamped on her passport. So simple! The nearest Brazilian Consulate was in *Ciudad del Este* in Paraguay, another country. This meant that there was no nearby city within Argentina in the vicinity of the Iguasú Falls to get the Brazilian Visa, and we needed to go to a third country to get it! We got discouraged and enjoyed the view from the Argentinian side only.

After returning from Argentina, we planned a trip to Europe through a local travel agent. It included Spain, Italy and France and a part of Switzerland for fifteen days. The package included room and board, transportation within Europe plus the guided tour facilities with the tour who would travel with us throughout the trip from starting in Madrid till finishing in Paris. The cost was 3000USD per person. We found it quite reasonable, not too expensive, and bought the packages.

Our main tour guide during this trip to Europe was a young Brazilian girl who spoke both Spanish and English very well. She was a living delight in our group. She also brought her boyfriend to accompany her. And that was an addition in our enjoyment because he was a charming young gentleman always full of smile and lots of jokes, both in English and Spanish. Both were fluent in both the languages apart from their native tongue, Portuguese. We went to many places in Spain after landing in Madrid. The transportation throughout the fifteen-day trip was superb luxury buses with all the facilities inside, from toilets to TVs. Madrid, of course, the capital of Spain, had so many fascinating sights, including museums and arts galleries, and live shows in the evenings. But the two places that impressed me most were Barcelona and Toledo. The sidewalk cafés in "Las Ramblas" avenue of Barcelona were fantastic with tourists all around the world. Sitting by an open-air table for a drink and some snacks, you could hear so many languages from different surrounding tables!

Another thing in Barcelona was the Cathedral with its gorgeous religious architecture of the medieval era. Besides, the statue of Jesus Christ, sculpted by the famous artist Gaudis. That was the only sculpture of Jesus Christ in nude, very impressive expression of Jesus chiseled by the valiant sculptor!

I liked Toledo for its simplicity. A city of so much medieval history was not spoiled by "modernism". It had no skyscrapers, no underground trains, not even luxury-looking plazas for attracting the wave of modern tourist gangs. We walked a lot on foot for several hours, entering some small art galleries and historical museums that tell the stories of Toledo. We even had our lunch in a small restaurant that looked like a village hut. Beauty and grandeur of Toledo lie in its simple architecture of the mixed Spanish cum Arabic style. Here you can see the evidence from the art and building architecture of Toledo that the Arabs rules Spain for almost eight centuries! Not only in the arts and architecture but also in the Spanish language, the Arab influence is dominant which in fact enriched the language. It is the only romance language, including French, Italian, Portuguese, and old Romano that was highly influenced by an Oriental culture, except for Sanskrit which is the birthmother of Latin and hence the origin of all the other languages with Latin roots.

From Spain we entered Italy with our first stop in Venice. The water channels and the *gondolas* in Venice reminded me of Holland, especially the waterways in Amsterdam and Rotterdam. Matty was excited about her several rides on the gondolas, the narrow boats for sightseeing on the waterways of Venice. All of them were full of foreign / international tourists. We met some families from Venezuela who happened to be staying in the same hotel as ours. We met them again at dinner in the same hotel and had friendly, lively conversations. Everyone seemed to be elated about their gondola rides. The food was delicious with fresh fish and pasta.

From Venice we headed to Rome and stayed in a hotel near the Vatican. The nearby train station was huge, just like the one we saw in Buenos Aires. This shows the Italian influence in Argentina, not just in mass immigration of the Italians, but in its city architecture, its design and construction. Matty and I were interested in seeing closely the churches and cathedrals in Vatican. There were so many! We spent two consecutive days there, climbing all the way to the top of the St. Peter's Cathedral and watching its famous dome painted by Michelangelo. Then we visited *el sótano* where many of the precious relics were preserved very carefully. We could see some of the physical remains of San Francisco de Assis. I remembered that some other parts of the same saint were preserved in the cathedral of Goa in India. In another trip to India, Matty and I visited there with my mother.

The day we were leaving Rome, we had an early breakfast in the hotel. While having our good breakfast and I was talking to a Mexican couple sitting in front of me on the same table, Matty went up to get some orange juice from the buffet display only a few yards from our table. She drank her orange juice, and I finished the last bite left. When we all got up ready to leave for the bus waiting outside, Matty noticed that her purse was missing. The purse contained her most important documents, including her US passport, and most important her medicines that she needed to take daily. We reported immediately to our guide, the Brazilian girl, and she searched all over in the dining hall and informed at the hotel's main registration desk. I accompanied her and finally when nothing was found, we went to the front desk again, and gave our addresses and phone number, just in case they could find it just in time.

We were all in a hurry leaving for Florence, a day-long drive from Rome. Our group in the bus was very sympathetic and helpful. One couple used their cell phone to call long distance to her bank in Puerto Rico for cancelling Matty's credit cards. Once we reached our hotel in Florence, it was quite late for the office hours of the US Consulate. But the pharmacies were open. We went to the nearest one, and again they helped us enormously, searching for and finally finding the Italian equivalents of all the medicines that Matty used to consume daily. Both of us were much relieved of anxieties after getting the medicines!

We went back to our hotel room, took long showers, ate something in the hotel's restaurant itself, and tried to take a rest and sleep. It was very exhausting a day full of anxieties. Next morning in the very first hours, we took a cab and went to the US Consulate. The gentleman who attended us was sympathetic to the situation but not surprised. It looked like that a lot of American tourists face the same fate in Rome and come to the US Consulate in despair. Fortunately, I had our passport numbers noted separately in my notebook. The Consulate officer was very glad to get that passport number and assured that with that number he could make a temporary passport for traveling further. He asked us to take a passport picture at a nearby photoshop. He even gave us the instructions on how to get there in a taxi. Again, I realized that losing a handbag in Rome must be a very common affair, and the US Consulates throughout Italy must be helping the American travelers over decades. I remembered my younger years in Calcutta where stealing from the tourists was as bad as in Rome, or perhaps worse. The "pick pocketers" in Calcutta are notoriously noteworthy worldwide!

From the US Consulate office, we took a cab to the photoshop, as directed by the Consulate officer, got two copies of her picture, both stamped at the back and signed by the photographer, and quickly got back the Consulate. We handed over the photos to the officer and within 15 minutes of waiting, a warm, new passport of Matty was delivered in her hands. It was such a relief for both of us!

We missed the sight-seeing in Florence, but glad to recover Matty's daily medicines and her passport. The passport, although temporary, was validated for six months. Once in Puerto Rico, she applied for and got a more permanent passport for the next ten years. That new passport is still in use! Now that Matty got her passport and we could continue traveling for the rest of our tour in Europe, let me tell you a story about the efficient "Pick pocketers" in Calcutta/Kolkata. My paternal uncle told it to me.

My uncle was waiting at a bus stop in front of his house and the pick-pocketer was waiting there too. Both wanted to catch the next bus, my uncle for reaching his office and the pick-pocketer for stealing purses, moneybags, and such small items from the passengers within the crowded bus, mainly from the people who were standing and holding the upper rail with one hand. That pick-pocketer was a local young boy. My uncle knew him well, and asked him jokingly, "Show me how good a pick-pocketer you are!" The young man replied smilingly but with respect, "Yes, Sir, I'll pick pocket your moneybag from your trousers' pocket! You will see it missing when you get down from the bus." My uncle smiled back and replied, "OK, son. This is a challenge! I'll catch you while you'll try to slide your poor fingers into my pocket". Both went up into the next bus and were standing side by side in a fully packed standing isle during the office hours. My uncle was very careful all the time. In half an hour my uncle got down at the bus stop in front of his office. The pick-pocketer got down too. They smiled at each other. My uncle shouted at him, "You loser, couldn't do anything you wanted. You couldn't pick my moneybag out from my trousers' pocket." The boy smiled, again very respectfully, and replied, "Of course, I picked it out of your pocket. Then, after a few minutes, I put it back into your pocket, thinking that you might need money to buy your lunch during the break!"

Back to our trip from Florence, we took the southern coastal highway to Monaco, the city-state famous for its casinos. Guided by our tour guides, we entered a casino. We had to keep everything, including passports, in a locked compartment that looked like a P.O. Box in the US. Then we entered and the space was full of people, coin operated machines and gambling tables. One thing I noticed was that there were no policepersons in uniform. Maybe there were many plain-clothed police. Matty played at a coin-operated machine for the twenty US Dollars we converted in local currency for gambling. I didn't gamble (nothing to do with religions!) but always stayed beside her to check the numbers and the coins. I used to enjoy it as an observer! Here, in Monaco, I did the same, and to my surprise, at the end Matty own some money! When she converted the local coins, she collected them at the end and got it converted at the Casino's cash register, it was over thirty Dollars! She was delighted. Me too.

After a short stay and a late lunch in Monaco, we followed the southern coastal route, passing by Marseille and Montpellier, and entered in the furthermost north-east corner of Spain. Here the Pyrenees Mountain ranges start and divide Spain from France all the way to its northwest end, thus protecting Spain from the cold winter winds of France. Northern Spain has a lovely, almost Mediterranean weather due to the existence of the Pyrenees mountains. The same way the Himalayas protect northern India from the cold wind of the Goby desserts in China. Along the hilly highway bordering

Spain from France by the Pyrenees, the first country state we passed by was Andorra, the smallest independent country on our planet! This highway parallel with the mountain ranges with its sharp twists and turns finally took us to the northern coast of Spain, and we reached Bilbao for overnighting. Next morning, after a heavy breakfast of Spanish omelet and baked potato plus toast and freshly brewed coffee, we headed again to France, passing by Lourdes, and entered in Bordeaux, the famous place for many brands of French wines, both red and white. We strolled around the city, enjoyed good wine and good food in dinner and watched French TV programs before going to bed.

Next morning again we had an early breakfast, for Bordeaux to Paris was a long drive that would take the entire day. This time Matty and I were more careful about not losing our handbags again like in Rome. We reached Paris nearly at sunset, went to our scheduled hotel and registered for our respective rooms. It was a big group registering simultaneously, and there were several girls at the desk helping us with our passport registration and the other formal details. We would be staying in Paris a few more days before flying back to America. This was our last stop in the City of Lights, and we were all very happily excited during registration. I tried to show off with my little French, and the young lady registering me laughed and laughed. I told her, "I'll sing a song instead!" She said, "OK, go ahead!" And I sang a song that Michelle taught me at Waterloo in 1965, imagine! After so many decades, I could still remember the melody but maybe failed in the lyrics. But the lady at the desk liked it, and even "Congratulated" me for singing in French! This helped us to get the room keys quickly. We checked into our room. It was small but neat. After taking a relaxing hot shower, we felt so good after some ten hours of driving that we changed our clothes to fresher ones, and went down to the restaurant on the ground floor for dinner. We were hungry! As we opened the entrance door of the restaurant and got inside, it was humming with people, mostly from our group.

The weather was so gorgeous next morning that right after breakfast we drove to the Garden of Versailles, rather than strolling inside the city. We would be here a few more days anyway, and to take advantage of the lovely weather we decided to see that famous garden first before any unfortunate and sudden rain arrived. The garden was wonderful, indescribably serene, full of lushes of green at this time of the year. There were lots of flower-work with a mosaic of many colors on the background of deep green grass, meticulously cut and arranged. Matty and I signed our names with the date on a big stone that was specially placed there, I thought, for the enthusiastic and excited tourists. I saw many names in different alphabets that I could not decipher. Some looked like Arabic but could also be Persian (Farsi) or Urdu. Similarly, my ignorance could not distinguish among Japanese, Chinese, or Korean. But it was fun!

Next day we went to see some of the most talked about tourist spots of the City of Lights: The Eiffel Tower, Montmartre, and the famous Cathedral of Sacre Coeur. Each one is famous by its own right in the history of France! Naturally, we took many pictures of and around the Eiffel Tower but couldn't go up since the elevator was in repair. We were a bit disappointed. When are we coming again to Paris to take a snapshot of the city from the top of the tower? We would have liked to show it to our grandchildren.

The Cathedral of Sacre Coeur (Sacred Heart) was immense in its dimension as well as in its architectural beauty. There were no ways I could describe it in words! One had to see it to appreciate its serenity. We went to Montmartre in the evening. There were small square tables, and four chairs at each table. They were wooden sets, but all painted in deep red. We ate our dinner there with a glass of French wine. Matty had dry white wine and I preferred red. From there we went to Moulin Rouge to get two tickets for us for the show. We were lucky to get them for the next evening. It was okey since we would be staying a couple of days more.

The weather continued to be good. Next morning, we visited some of the famous places, like Place de la Concord. It was amazing to see how the traffic circulated around that place. The wide boulevard passes through and under the famous arch: Porte de la Chapelle. In the afternoon we visited several other historical sights. The same evening, we went to see the show at Moulin Rouge. It started at 8PM. We reached the area at around 6PM and had a nice leisurely candle-lit dinner at a nearby restaurant. The environment under dim light and soft background music was coolly romantic. In Paris, romance and dance have no timing. We checked in the theater a bit earlier than 8PM even though the seats were numbered and reserved as in any performance hall. We just wanted to have a warming up time for ourselves before the show started. If I can remember correctly, it was a comic skit, very humorous, but I can't recollect the details today after so many decades.

The day we had the return flight from Paris to San Juan with a short stopover in Madrid, the tour organizers arranged a taxi for taking us to Orlay International Airport after our breakfast in the hotel. Our Brazilian tour guide and her boyfriend gave us a big farewell hug. She whispered, "It is not a goodbye hug; it is *'Hasta Luego'*!" This melted our hearts!

She was so nice to us throughout the trip and took special care when Matty lost her bag in Rome. We will always remember her as a good guide and as a great friend.

Since we were flying from east to west, crossing the Atlantic Ocean, we saved time, and arrived in San Juan by 4 PM local hour. The flight was smooth with no turbulence at all, and the on-flight service of food and drinks was excellent. As always, we took a cab from the San Juan International Airport Luis Muñoz Marin straight to our home in Mayagüez. The cab driver was a middle-aged lady. Matty sat beside the driver's seat, and they kept conversing over our Europe tour throughout the two-hours trip. We had very limited luggage, only a carry-on suitcase and a handbag for each one, plus a few souvenirs we bought for us and for our family, especially the grandkids. The driver lady helped us to get the luggage into our living room. Matty prepared some coffee for the three of us, accompanied with some sweet crackers (that was all we had at home as we were away for two weeks!). The driver lady thanked her many times before leaving. Matty advised her to drive carefully. It would be again another two-hours' drive for her alone to reach safely in San Juan. Matty is always very hospitable with the drivers and treated them with coffee and some snacks whenever we travelled from San Juan to Mayagüez. This is very nice of her, a way of appreciation, giving a sincere tip valued more than money!

After returning from Europe, life became quiet as usual. My teaching duties were normal. Matty had her regular work as an Administrative Personnel in the Office of Graduate Studies. We used to spend most of our spare time in Rotary Club, the Alumni Association of UPRM and in the Club for Office Workers and the Association of the Students' parents, four clubs in a row!. The first time I joined Rotary Club was in

Venezuela in 1977 and then continued attending Rotary Club meetings when we returned to Kingston, Canada. When I moved to Puerto Rico, one of the English professors, Dr. Robert Sherwin, introduced me to the Rotary Club of Mayagüez. I joined the club as a regular member again and Matty followed me. After several years of regular attendance and service, we both became Paul Harris Fellow, an honor in Rotary. We also attended the Rotary International Conventions in Atlanta, USA and in Toronto, Canada. We registered for the same convention in Hamburg, Germany, but couldn't make it for some health issues.

Besides Rotary International Conventions in Atlanta and Toronto, we also attended two engineering conferences in Cuba in 2016 and 2018. It was exciting, starting from the visa requirement and other formalities for our US passports. I have both the US and the Canadian passports but while travelling with Matty I prefer to use my US passport for not standing in two separate lines while checking in a foreign country. In Cuba, for example, a Canadian passport wouldn't need a visa stamp; but like in Brazil, in Cuba also the US passports need a tourist visa to enter.

Both the times, the conference was in Havana, a very beautiful city on the oceanside and full of Spanish architecture in the old part of the city. The new central area of Havana was, of course, full of new government buildings and plazas decorated with the glories of Castro's revolution, and the statues of Fidel Castro and Ché Guevara, and quotes from their speeches engraved in huge letters all over in the immense space around the central *Plaza de la Revolución*. There were also words from José Martí, the poet and the great Cuban hero in public education. During our first visit to Cuba in 2016, we met many delegates from Europe, mainly from France and Germany, during the technical sessions and the social get-togethers of the conference. Apart from the technical sessions in Engineering and Architecture, there were several cultural activities with music and dance.

During our second trip to Cuba in 2018, we met a senior professor from Germany who happened to work in the same area of manufacturing engineering as mine. We met at lunch every day during the conference, and later kept in touch through correspondence till he retired. Through that connection I sent a student of mine to Germany in his institute for further training and Graduate studies. Both the trips to Cuba were very satisfying and educational for us. In Puerto Rico, because of the travel restrictions from the US government, we have very little firsthand experience in Cuba. These two trips to Havana open our eyes and our minds as well. A Puerto Rican poet, Doña Lola Rodríguez de Tío, once wrote: "Cuba and Puerto Rico are the two wings of a bird". Indeed, due to cultural affinity, people share their ideas more than ever. I could see that in Matty during these two trips. She felt so much at home in Havana, as much as in Buenos Aires or Barcelona, that she could make more friends simply talking in her own language, telling them some Puerto Rican stories, and even local jokes. My eldest son, Kumar, also had a chance to visit Havana on a work assignment from Canada. He is bilingual in English and Spanish and enjoyed very much the social evenings in Havana as well as working with the Cuban colleagues. The organizer of both the international events was Dr. Orestes Santiago, a professor of Engineering. He came here for a visit, and we got acquainted both professionally and socially. Dr. Gerson Beauchamp, a colleague in the Electrical Engineering Department, and a great friend of mine since I came to Puerto Rico in 1989, organized both the trips to

Cuba, including registration, travel and hotel reservation. Each time we took some students with us who presented their research papers at the conferences. Apart from purely technical sessions, there were special sessions on Engineering Education. I was lucky enough to present my work in both the technical and the educational sessions. That way I had a chance to meet people from the Faculties of Education in Cuba and from other countries. We met delegates from Brazil, Argentina, Colombia, and several other Latin American countries. There was also participation from Canada.

You could see on the streets of Havana many cars of old models of the fifties and sixties but very well maintained. We used to take taxis to go to the downtown districts and then walked around. We attended Sunday Mass in the cathedral and met the priest after the mass. What a coincidence! The same priest was in Mayagüez, and he could recognize us, and we could remember him conducting mass in the Cathedral of Mayagüez. The most interesting part of the priest was that he was an English-speaking American priest living in Cuba for years.

Both the times, we stayed with a typically local family of Havana who rented their spare rooms. That way we could have a feel of the middle-class family life in Havana. We used to have our daily breakfast with some of the family members before going to the conference. The second time in 2018 we stayed with the same family, and this time really felt like friends of that family. It was also much less expensive than staying at a standard hotel in Havana. Thanks to my friend Gerson for making such a nice and lasting connection with the residents of Havana. There were no such events in almost the last three years since 2019 due to the pandemic COVID-19, but we would love to attend again if there would be such a convention in November 2022. Now, today is December 28, 2022, but no technical conference was organized in Havana, similar to the last two we attended. Hopefully, we will be able to attend one in 2023!

Matty and I visited Colombia three times in 2016, 2017 and 2019. Since I lived in Colombia for almost three years (1970 – 72) in my younger years, I was genuinely interested to show my wife the country and its people that I admire so much. The occasions (and my excuses!) were the Latin American Conferences in Mechanical Engineering. The first one in 2016 took place in Cali, at the University Del Valle, where I worked many moons ago! We flew to Bogotá and stayed there for several days. There were so many things to see in Bogotá! The most attractive of all was the Gold Museum (Museo del Oro) that has a great historical importance, from the Pre-Columbian era of the Amerindians till the end of the Spanish colonial era, on the art and engineering of how the gold was extracted from the mines till photofinishing it to elegant jewelry. Another worth seeing spot was the Cathedral of Salt (Catedral de la Sal) in *Zipaquirá*. It was amazing to see the solid structures made from natural mineral salt of the rocks! We visited an ex-Amerindian village in *Fusagasugá* and bought some colorful and long ponchos (in Colombia and Venezuela the name is *ruana*). I remember that I bought the same type of punchos, *Ruanas Boyacenses,* for Eligia and me, a red one for her and a blue one for me, some five decades ago! Bogotá used to be very cold year-round for its height, just like La Paz of Bolivia, and you could see a small group people, wearing poncho/ruana, at each street corner after the sunset, relaxing after a full working day and gossiping on the talk of the town, with a few shots of *aguardiente blanco or aguardiente crístal,* a local liquor simply differentiated by its brand name. Today, due to the increasing effects of global warming and atmospheric pollution as well as an increase in population, Bogotá is not that cold anymore.

From Bogotá we flew into Cali, *La Sultana del Valle* (The Sultan of the Valley) because it lies in the heart of the Cauca Valley, a very attractive location. We had a hotel reservation right on the edge of the university campus. Now there are many hotels around the campus since the campus had grown enormously over the last couple of decades. Once we checked into our room, I started connecting by phone calls with my old colleagues, friends, and most importantly, with the organizers of the conference. The ME Chairperson, Dr. John Jairo was my student at UPRM where he did his master's degree and then a Doctorate in Brazil. John came to our hotel right away, accompanied by his girlfriend, Norita, and took us out for dinner in the most attractive part of the city, *La Ermita*. It was an open-air restaurant, and you could hear the murmuring ripples of the river flowing past the edge of the restaurant. We had a long and very relaxing evening with John and Norita recollecting his two years of study in Mayagüez, and I was telling them the stories of my first teaching assignment at the university in Cali. Matty liked Norita very much for her open-mindedness, and they became very good friends right at their first encounter in that evening. We spent over two hours in that riverside restaurant. Then they drove us back to our hotel and we had a great goodnight's rest.

Next day the conference started. After our breakfast we walked to the campus. The Mechanical Engineering complex, the venue of the conference, was not too far from our hotel. I still remember the small two-storied building when we moved there in 1972! Now there are several other buildings but none of them are higher than two floors. The entire campus now was beautifully spread over a carpet of deep green grass, and there were no skyscrapers anywhere in my sight. There were now several small cafeterias rather than a huge dining hall. Later, we went to see several new buildings constructed over the last half a century since I left Cali. One of them was named after Dr. Alberto León Betancourt, who was my Dean of Engineering during 1970 – 72. Another hall of the new ME building was dedicated to Professor Claudio Fernández, who was the ME Chairperson, and my direct boss. Memories revived, and Matty and I laid some flowers in those two places in honor of their departing soul, and especially I felt nostalgic remembering their friendship and kind behavior with me.

The four days of the conference were hectic. One early morning, we were surprised to get a call from the lobby and hurriedly got down because the girl at the reception desk informed us that someone was in the lobby wanting to visit us. We saw a lady sitting on a sofa in the lobby. When we faced her, to my utter surprise, it was Vicky, who was a student in Chemical Engineering and a good friend of my friend Manuel Quintana, a young and bright faculty member, when I started working there. It was such a pleasant "shock" to meet her again after some five decades. Once I introduced Matty to Vicky, they became good friends almost instantly. They felt good vibes. From that day on, when I was busy at the conference sessions, Vicky used take Matty out in her VW to show the worth seeing spots of the city and to invite her for good Colombian coffee and the typical *arepas* filled with cheese. In the evening, the three of us went out several times in Vicky's car to have our dinner in the nicest areas of Cali. One such spot was in front of the cathedral *La Ermita* and across the small stream of water, a rivulet that cut across that part of the city. The place was called *El Pilón*, a small restaurant that served only typical Colombian plates. We ordered *sobrebarriga*, a thick *churrasco* from the stomach of a cow. Vicky also took us to several new museums and a brand-new Gold Museum that didn't exist before when I lived there.

Once the conference was over, Matty and I did some touring around Cali, visiting the *Calima* lake and then the mountain town of *Sílvia*. One early morning we hired a taxi that took us to Popayán in the adjacent province of Cauca. Popayán was popularly called the 'white city' (la *ciudad blanca*) because most of the public and government buildings in its downtown areas were painted white, and also because it was a very religious center of Christianity. White being the color of purity in Christian faith and that of peace in all faiths, Popayán remained as the White City even today. The building architecture around the city center was quite attractive but all in white color. The central plaza in the middle, the white cathedral on one side, the government's municipal building in white plaster on its opposite and the main priest's residence adjacent to the cathedral, looked like a typical Spanish setting of a small town in the colonial time.

Next year the same conference took place in Manizales, a mountain town in Colombia. This time Matty and I flew straight from Bogotá to Manizales and didn't spend overnight in Bogotá. Curiously, like last year in Cali, we got a hotel right on campus. It was only a five-minute walk from the venue of the conference. It was a small hotel, well-furnished and very good breakfast of local taste with eggs and cheese-filled arepas and fantabulous coffee! Manizales lies in the heart of the coffee growing regions of Colombia. So, it serves the best coffee of Colombia! We used to get down to the hotel's cafeteria after getting ready quite early in the morning. Often, we were the first in the cafeteria. The breakfast was a buffet system, so that you could serve yourself on the plate all you want, except that the coffee was served by the waitress at the time you wanted it. The waitresses were very friendly, and Matty used to take her time leisurely, conversing with the waitresses and sipping her delicious coffee. I had to run to the conference starting at 8 AM sharp and she used to join me later with no hurry at all.

A group of student delegates came from Cali whom we happened to know only a year before. John Jairo couldn't come but he sent Joao, the Associate Director who also went to Brazil with John Jairo for his Doctorate degree. Colombia had always a good academic exchange program with Brazil over many decades. The program was there even when I worked at the University Del Valle in Cali during 1970 – 72. At that time the university in Cali didn't have a master's program in engineering, and the fresh faculty members were sent to Brazil, mainly at the Polytechnic of Sao Paolo or at the Catholic University in Rio. My good friend, Camilo Botero, with whom I used to do regular jogging up to the hills of *Siloé* in Cali, did his graduate studies in Sao Paulo. Several other Colombian colleagues with whom I worked later in Venezuela did their master's degrees in Rio. Horacio Rey, Carlos Rey worked with me in San Cristóbal, and Carlos Alberto Sosa was my colleague in Mérida. They all did their Doctoral studies in Brazil. At the University of Manizales, one of the organizers of the conference, Dr. Ing. Sebastián Durango did his Doctorate in Engineering in Karlsruhe, Germany. Colombia always had very good academic exchange programs with the European universities. In Manizales, we walked up the hilly areas and all the way to the top where there was a tall statue of Jesus Christ, *El Cristo Rey*, and a nice, cozy cafeteria. After walking a lot, especially climbing the hill, we used to feel hungry and used to take our early dinner right there instead of taking it in the same hotel. *Variety is the spice of life!*

In November 2019, the same conference, *Congreso Iberoamericano de Ingeniería Mecánica (CIBIM)*, again took place in Colombia, this time in Cartagena, a tourist attraction on the northern coast. Cartagena was a city of historical significance during independence from the Spaniards and hence, the end of the colonial era. Cartagena is also close to Barranquilla, the big, industrial city and Santa Marta, another tourist spot of *La Sierra Nevada*. Besides attending the conference, we went to see several places of attraction. *El Castillo de San Felipe* was one of them. The labyrinths within the castle were extraordinary. You could hear a sound struck at one end of the tunnel from its opposite end. There was a show in the evening outside the castle in the open air, *Sonido y Luz,* that described the history of the castle from the colonial period till today, with an extraordinary collage of light and sound. The show took about an hour and a half!

Another day we went to see *El Popa*. It was a special area, quite high but on the edge of the Caribbean Sea. During the Pre-Columbian period, the Amerindian chiefs used to throw their prisoners from that high spot into the sea to be fed by the crocodiles. Probably the Conquistadores from Europe did the same to the Amerindians! Who knows? Now a days El Popa has become a place of tourist attraction.

During that week in Cartagena, selection and coronation of the beauty queen, Miss Colombia, was going on in the same hotel Hilton where we were staying. That way we could see the ceremony firsthand and had a chance to personally know some of the contestants from different provinces of Colombia. Matty, being extraordinarily extrovert and conversant, made friendship with the "queens" of Del Valle (Cali!) and Tolima

(Ibagué). I was familiar with both places. Ibagué is the capital city of Tolima where Harold, son of Doña Chila lived; and I used to go there occasionally for eating the delicious *Tamales Tolimences*. Also, there was once the Annual Convention of the Society of Engineers of Colombia in Ibagué, and I took part, representing the University Del Valle. I still remember the beautiful music presented by the Choir of the cathedral of Ibagué. It was a memorable evening!

Apart from sightseeing and the conference, Matty and I did some shopping in downtown Cartagena. Being a city of tourist attractions, shopping was all over. We bought some souvenirs, as always, plus a small broach of real emerald (there were many fake ones!) for Hanny, Matty's daughter, and a necklace of the same material for Matty. We both liked Cartagena very much and flew back to San Juan through Bogotá. There was always a feeling of nostalgia. Hanny and Paco (Hanny's husband) came to the airport in San Juan to pick us up, and that was a great relief for me, as I didn't have to drive back to Mayagüez, some two and half hours behind the steering wheel, and especially at night. It was on the same day as Hanny's birthday, and I felt genuinely happy while handing over to her the birthday gift, a broach of genuine emerald!

Our longest trip, farthest from Puerto Rico, was to India. We planned it in such a way that we could see a few things in northern India, like the famous Taj Mahal, before coming to see my family in Kolkata. On our way to Delhi, we stopped very shortly in Heathrow airport in London, changed flight to an Indian airline, Jet Air. The layover time at Heathrow was very long, almost twelve hours, and we had our breakfast, lunch and dinner at the airport itself in the same restaurant. That way we became much familiar and friendly with the waiters and waitresses of the restaurant. When we arrived at Delhi airport, to our surprise we realized that none of our checked-in luggage had arrived that included most of our necessary items and some gifts for our family members. Fortunately, Matty's medicines were in her carry-on bag. We didn't have to go through the same worries as in Rome and Florence where she lost everything including her passport and the medicines. The airline was very generous. They gave us some cash, quite a handsome one, for buying the essential items till the baggage arrived. After checking into our hotel, when we went out on the street again, we took a three-seated "scooter" to the downtown Connaught Circle to do some shopping for the essential items with the money that the airline gave us. It was the first time Matty had a ride on a three-seater. She was excited. In the shopping area she was overwhelmed to see so many new things that are typically Indian, like the long *Sari* as a lady's dress, and especially the Indian style jewelry. Of course, we didn't buy jewelry from the money that the airline donated us! Matty even made friends with some of the salesgirls despite the language barriers. She became very happy to talk to them in her broken, spoken English, and they too enjoyed talking with her. Matty is very white, almost Swedish blonde, and that was attractive in our Indian culture as a foreign lady! Cultural Colonialism from two centuries of British rule!

Next day the luggage arrived! We were relieved of our anxieties of losing everything. We went out to see the tourists' areas of Delhi. There were so many! Some of them were the Gandhi Memorial shrine, the beautiful Bahai temple, and some of the areas in the Old Delhi section as well, like *Kuttab Minar, Jumma Mosque* and many other areas of tourist attraction. We did our sightseeing all day, came back to the hotel in the evening, and had our dinner right there. We were very tired from walking and especially for Matty, the excitement of seeing totally new places and their people. We went up to our room, took showers and sank into our bed with delicious slumber.

Next morning, we woke up late, had our breakfast in the hotel's restaurant and took a cab to see my cousin, *Deepak*, and his family. I hadn't seen him since I left India in 1962! Now he has a family, and we were delighted to meet his wife and grown-up children. His wife took Matty out for some nearby sightseeing while I chilled with my cousin. There were so many things to talk about after so many years of absence! We spent all day with them. Matty had a good idea about our family environment. This was the first time she was fully absorbing the newness of a totally different Asian culture, and I could see that she was enjoying it with my cousin's family. Both Deepak and Matty were very extrovert and open-minded types, never afraid of a foreign environment, language or culture!

Our hotel had a travel bureau on its ground floor near the lobby. Next morning, I went there and booked a package tour that included Agra, where the famous Taj Mahal was the greatest attraction, plus the cities of historical importance and tourist attractions in Rajasthan, namely, Jaipur and Udaipur. That day, after booking the travel package, we spent the whole day, again in the downtown Connaught Circle, visiting some art galleries and, of course, some shopping malls. These huge malls were new to me, since they didn't exist in Kolkata, or in any other big city in India for that matter, in 1961. Matty was delighted to shop around in the Indian style dress stores, trying to fit our Indian style *kurta* and *salwar*.

Next morning, we packed up our initial belongings, plus whatever a few things and a handful of souvenirs we bought in

Delhi and got into a private taxi arranged by our travel agent. The day was nice and cool, and the taxi driver was friendly. We headed for Agra. The highway was clean and with divided four lanes, nothing to envy our American roads. Within a couple hours we were already in Agra. We had a reservation at Agra Hilton, and it had a great location. We could see the Taj Mahal from our room's window. I was in Agra before when we went to an NCC (National Cadet Corps) training there in my college years. That was during our NCC Summer Camp in 1958, many decades ago! Matty was highly impressed by the majestic charm of Taj Mahal, a tall structure of milk-white marble. We saw it again at night. It was a full-moon night, and the moonlight flooding over the white marble was truly a hypnotic beauty. It is difficult to describe with words. You must see it with your own eyes to admire the Taj Mahal on a full-moon night.

Agra is full of historical buildings of the Mughal empire. The following day we visited some of them. Diwan-I-Am and Diwan-I-Khas were the two stone-structured palaces where the emperors used to have their administrative centers and pleasure gardens. Emperor Shah Jahan, who built Taj Mahal, was imprisoned by his own son Aurangzeb, in one of those palaces. The old, banished king could see Taj Mahal from one of the windows of the palace. Taj Mahal was a token of true love for his queen, MumTaj who gave him ten children. In the underground history of a great work of art there is always a sad story. It was rumored that Shah Jahan killed the main architect of Taj Mahal so that he wouldn't be able to design and build another similar or better structure. Such stories, rumor or fact, nobody knows, but are always embedded in all the ancient great architectural wonders like the Pyramids and the Sphinx of Egypt, the Mayan Pyramids of Chichen-Itza and Tulúm, the Aztec Pyramids of Teotihuacán in Mexico or the Incan city of Machu Pichu in Peru.

We stayed a couple of days more in Agra. There was another modern building, still under construction over decades, that intends to compete with Taj Mahal. This was in Dayal Bag, near Agra. The story goes that rich merchants of India want to build another Taj Mahal. History says that Taj Mahal was built in twenty-two years. The monument in Dayal Bag is not yet finished. It might take a century! All the ancient architectural wonders worldwide were built with support from forced labor of thousands of slaves and prisoners. The owners of Dayal Bag can't afford that today!

After Agra, we went to Fatehpur Sikri where the great emperor, Akbar, Shah Jahan's grandfather, built his glory. Even the ruins are spectacular! The wall surrounding the city is a marvel in architectural design even today. There were many other smaller tourist spots around Agra and Fatehpur Sikri that we hopscotched on our way to Jaipur and Udaipur in Rajasthan. The same driver with the same car accompanied us all the way. In the beginning, he was a bit hesitant to sit and eat with us, a typical example of our notorious caste system of India! But with my insistence and Matty's charming friendliness, he became more comfortable with us. He even started relating Indian jokes in Hindi that I had to translate in Spanish for Matty!

Jaipur is called the "Red City" because it is surrounded by a circular red wall and most of the public office buildings of the local government are red. The enormous wall has five gates for entering the city. I could imagine *Rana Pratap Singh* entering the city through one of its gates with his cavalry and the citizens were in long files bowing down to greet the great victorious king who fought ferociously against the Muslim emperor of his time. This reminded me of a parallel scene in Venezuela. Simon Bolivar entering the town of Boconó (where Eligia was born!) and the ladies – the housewives – came out on the balconies to greet him, and the *Libertador* looked up to see them and uttered, "This is the garden of Venezuela"! In Sanskrit we say *"Birabhogya Basundhara"*, roughly translating it means: Even Mother Nature loves to be seduced by the heroes! We stayed at an Indian style hotel in Jaipur, named Shahpur House, and the weather was so nice that the dinner was served in the open area on the terrace of the building. There we met many European tourists, mainly young couples. Being Indian, I am used to hot and spicy food, but Matty can't stand it because it spoils her stomach, and hence her appetite. In the hotel's kitchen, they used to make light food for her, and the chef would personally bring it to her. If he were busy, he would smile at her and loudly utter, "Madam, your baked potato with oregano is ready!" She was very well treated in all the meals in Shahpur House. Such personal touches are rare in the hotels of America, no matter five-star, deluxe or premium in standard. But Matty and I had experienced similar hospitality in small places like in tourist areas of Puerto Plata in Dominican Republic. There also the kitchen chef used to keep ready the freshly prepared *Mangú* (a typical Dominican dish of mashed plantain with spices!) for Matty at breakfast.

From Jaipur we went to Udaipur and stayed in a government hostel, like our *Airbnb* of today. It was very well maintained and much cheaper than any private hotel. I was really surprised by the cleanliness of the place. Once in Udaipur, I called the family of Dr. Vikram Pandya, one of my colleagues in Puerto Rico. Vikram's parents and younger brother came to our hostel immediately and took us to their home to meet the other members of their family. There we met Vikram's sister-in-law (his brother's wife) and their little daughter. They spoke mainly Hindi, some English and no Spanish, but Matty didn't feel any language problem. She found in them their open-mindedness and delight in meeting new people. Both of us were very impressed by their friendliness.

Next morning Vikram's father came and took us on a tour of the city. Our driver was always with us, and while driving, Vikram's father sitting by the driver's side in the front, gave us a guided tour of the city. Udaipur looked like a very clean and well-maintained historical city. We didn't find any garbage on the streets, which is rather a rare example in Indian cities. Then he took us to the main castle of Udaipur and became our tour guide for a walking tour throughout the castle. It took about two hours as he started explaining the history at every stop. Later I realized that he worked there and only recently retired. That is why he introduced us to many of his ex-colleagues from the castle.

Vikram's brother was also with us during our four or five days stay in Udaipur. Several times his wife and daughter took us to parks and other open-air sightseeing spots, like fountains and small waterfalls on the outskirts of Udaipur. We found them very enthusiastic in showing us around every detail of their loving historical city they felt so proud of! On our way back from Udaipur to Delhi, we stayed one night in Chittor, another glorious city of the Rajput Empire. Unlike Jaipur, this city was a *"blue city"*, full of blue-washed government buildings and palaces. We went touring some of them and met a friendly Japanese tourist. He was touring India with his young son of about twelve years old. We shared our travel experience with him, and he showed much interest in visiting Latin America someday. He expressed interest in learning Spanish. I told him that I took a course in Japanese at the university and worked with a Japanese colleague for one year. Then we two exchanged a few words of greetings in Japanese!

The return trip from Chittor to Delhi was relatively shorter as we didn't have to go through Agra. India had by now many divided highways with excellent pavement quality. We didn't see any accident throughout the trip of two weeks on different roads and highways. We stayed in Delhi a few more days. We visited my cousin again and they were delighted to see us. His wife took us to do more sightseeing, this time more in Old Delhi. We liked so much the serene beauty of peace and silence in *Gandhi Sharani* and in the Bahai Temple that we took my sister-in -law there. She must have seen these two spots many times but was glad to be accompanied by us. On the last day in Delhi, we finally discharged our driver. He was with us for two weeks all the time and we developed a bond of friendship. We felt nostalgic as he said goodbye, got into the car and the car slowly disappeared in morning fog at the bent of the street outside our hotel. It was not easy to forget a travelling partner. After he left, we went up to our room and started packing for our next trip, a straight flight from Delhi to Kolkata.

We had reservation in a modest Airbnb, like the one in Udaipur, in Ballygunge area in South Kolkata, not too far from our paternal home, the place where I spent the first twenty years of my life before leaving for Germany on February 12, 1962. I still remember that date! My grandma called it *"Agastya Jatra" (the journey of Agastya)* since she had the hunch that I wouldn't return to India to settle down. She was right!

Matty and I spent a couple of days sightseeing on our own before meeting my family, for I knew very well that once in the family we would have very little opportunity to see things on our own. I know the Indian customs very well. We went to see the Victoria Memorial Hall, also of white marble. The British called it the Taj Mahal of Calcutta. It was a nice building after the name of Queen Victoria of England, but nothing to compare with the majestic beauty of Taj Mahal. I asked Matty: If Taj Mahal gets ten points, how many points would you give to Victoria Memorial Hall. First, she nodded her head, smiled, winked at me, and replied: Six! The surroundings of the hall were excellent with low cut grass field where you would see the lovers walking slowly and the kids strolling by themselves or playing with the adult members of their families. The pace is slow, relaxed, and often romantic. Right across the Victoria Memorial Hall, within five hundred yards, stands the majestic St. Paul's Cathedral. It also had a large compound of well-maintained green grass. Matty, being a devoted Catholic, loved the surroundings and eagerly entered. Wow, what an internal architecture, nothing to be envied about the St. Peter's in the Vatican! Matty walked around and observed all the minute details and was very impressed.

The entire surroundings of the Victoria Memorial Hall and the St. Paul's Cathedral was in the heart of Kolkata, in a much wider and open area called the *Maidan* meaning 'field'. There was a tall tower within a short distance in the Maidan, called the Monument, like the Kuttab Minar we visited in Delhi. Again, the Monument as compared to the Kuttab Minar was like the Victoria Memorial Hall compared with the Taj Mahal. The British tried to compete with the Mughal Empire in India but couldn't succeed. The Maidan is called the "Lungs of Kolkata" since its wide-open space helps reduce the air pollution of the metropolis. We couldn't get to the top of the tower as the elevator was under repair. We walked around for a bit more sightseeing in the Maidan area where we saw the soccer fields of the well-known Clubs of Calcutta, like Mogan Mohan, Muhammadan Sporting and East Bengal. Then we walked to my paternal home. It was only about half an hour's walk from the Maidan, but the entire strolling and sightseeing in the Maidan, including the Victoria Memorial Hall, St. Paul's Cathedral, the Monument, the soccer fields, etc. took over two hours. We were tired but excited to meet our family. For Matty, it would be the first time to see my mom and my sisters!

As we knocked at the main entrance door, it immediately opened, as I could see they were all waiting for us to see my "New" wife. My mom embraced Matty without many formalities for introduction. Later she introduced Matty to my two sisters, Mina, and Bandana, my two nephews, Babai and Ankur, and Babai's recently married wife, Nivedita. We all sat in our main living room and shared our feelings of getting together finally as a family with joy and excitement. Everybody wanted to talk, especially with Matty, and I was the only translator. We all talked and talked, and time passed so fast that we didn't notice that it was already lunch time. We all moved to our small eating area adjacent to the kitchen. The smell of fish curry was already in the air. I felt so good and Matty noticed that sniffing aroma in the air. Eight of us squeezed around the relatively small dining table. My sister Bandana served the meal. I sat beside Matty explaining to her each food item. She was already familiar with some of them since I used to cook while living at Cesaní building in Mayagüez and she used to come for tasting.

As usual, neighbors, friends and relatives came to visit us, and we also visited some of them during the first week of our stay in Kolkata. It was wonderful to see some of them after so many decades! Then we planned a trip to Goa, an ex-colony of Portugal that the Indian government "annexed" after its independence. My mother, my sister Bandana and her husband, Netaji agreed to accompany us. The other sister Mina and her husband, Jahar, couldn't come for other family commitments. I arranged the trip through a local travel agent, the same way I did in Delhi for our trip to Agra and Rajasthan. Only this time I didn't reserve a car or a driver since we would be staying in one place only on the seabeach.

The flight was short with a stopover in Mumbai (Bombay, the earlier name). The hotel in Goa was a four-star one, like the one in Jaipur. The package included all meals and snacks. In sum, it was a trip designed for relaxing in a family environment so that Matty could know my family well, and *vice versa*. There was no rush to get up early in the morning. The family breakfast was fabulous. Here Matty could get a taste of Goanese plates that had much Portuguese influence, which again resembled some Spanish and hence Latin American dishes. In sum, because of international tourism in Goa, we also had an international food menu. You could also get German *Schnitzel* and Hungarian *Gulash* in Goa!

After a heavy breakfast we used to go to the beaches daily. The hotel had its own private beach, but we preferred to walk a bit and then settle down on a public beach to meet more people and get a flavor of the local culture. We met tourists worldwide! My sister Bandana was very happy to have Matty with her and they walked a lot together. The language difference vanished! My mom accompanied them from time to time. Netaji and I just relaxed on the beach, drinking a few beers from time to time. Since Matty was not much used to spicy and hot food with chilies, the cook would make a special preparation of fish with oregano, ginger, and turmeric with no other spice, and he would make it ready for her as soon as she'd arrive at the dining table with us. We experienced the same cordial treatment before in Agra and Rajasthan!

The Cathedral of Goa was remarkable for its architecture and some parts of the body of the Saint San Francisco de Assis was buried there. At least that was the story the tour guide told us. My mother and Matty liked the Sunday Mass there in Portuguese. I enjoyed the setting of the ceremony although couldn't understand much of the sermon in Portuguese. I always thought that Portuguese was closer to Spanish and that I'd understand a good portion of the Mass. I was wrong! Probably Bengali, Assamese and Uria are much closer to one another than Spanish, Portuguese, and Italian. At least, these three European languages have the same scripts whereas our Indian languages have totally different letters in writing but there are much verbal and oral similarities.

We enjoyed our family vacation in Goa but couldn't travel to any other places of South India. I remember vividly that in another trip with my mother and Netaji, we traveled all the way to the southern tip of India, where the Arabian Sea, the Bay of Bengal and the Indian Ocean meet, and it is supposed to be a very auspicious point where the Vivekananda Rock lies within a stone's throw. My mom had no problem reaching the rock, crossing the little barriers of water. She was physically and mentally very fit for traveling long distances. We came back to Kolkata after spending a week in Goa. It was so delightful to have my sister and mother with us, and that way Matty felt very good to be a part of our family in India!

After returning to Kolkata, we spent another week visiting friends and relatives; some of them I hadn't met for ages. In Puerto Rico, the family bond is like that in India with many cousins and nephews and nieces to visit, and Matty felt that feeling in India just like in her hometown of Mayagüez and around in the little but enchanted island: *Borinquen,* the more authentic name of Puerto Rico before the Spaniards touched the island.

After returning from India, Matty and I made a few local trips within the island and in some of the neighboring countries like Costa Rica and Panama. In Costa Rica, we were entertained by Pablo and his girlfriend. Pablo was the brother of one of our students, Christian. So, Pablo took special care of us! He and his girlfriend showed us around the downtown of San José, the capital of Costa Rica. On one occasion he kept his car unlocked in the busy commercial center of San José and we all walked out. When I reminded him, "Pablo, you forgot to lock the car!" He smiled and replied," Oh, Jay, nothing dangerous happens here!"

No wonder Costa Rica is called Switzerland of the Americas. It is the most peaceful country in Latin America. Its president, Dr. Diego Arias received the Nobel Peace Prize. Many North Americans settle in Costa Rica after retirement. It is also the most eco-environmentally conscious country in Central America for which it is a great place of tourist attraction for ecotourism. Many tourists also come to see the live volcanos of *Poi* and others that can be seen from San José. We were lucky to observe the eruption of one of them right from our hotel in San José. It was really fascinating to observe how the lava was flowing down the slopes of the volcano and approaching the plains! I had never seen such a dramatic, dynamic show of nature!

There are many historical buildings in San José. The architecture of the Cathedral is famous and the second biggest in Latin America after the Cathedral of Buenos Aires in Argentina. There are many museums and art galleries all over in San José, resembling very much a Central European city like Cologne, Budapest, or Vienna. After spending a week in San José, and enjoying a musical show in its National Theater, equally famous for its architecture, we took a trip in the mountains and reached all the way to Cartago. It is a smaller town of medieval style in Europe. The weather of Cartago, due to its altitude, was cooler and much comfortable than in San José during the months of June and July.

Our next short tour was to Panama. I had passed through the international airport of Panama City many times en route Colombia and Peru but never stayed in Panamá before. It was my first trip with Matty to explore this small and beautiful country. Small is beautiful! Panama City was very cosmopolitan (and still is!). We found in Panama City many tourists from all over Europe and Asia, not just from USA and Canada. We stayed in two different hotels in two occasions, one when we reached Panama and the other on the way back. In both times, the impression was the same: A city beaming with tourism! Then we moved up north almost to the border of Costa Rica, touching and overnighting in the small towns of Amerindian habitation. Then we moved south as far as we could on highways and with available public transportation, all the way to the edges of the swamp region of *Chocó* in the northernmost Colombia. In that area, there are no roads. People usually take a boat ride to go to Colombia, either to Barranquilla, Cartagena or Santa Marta.

We found the Panamanian people very friendly, just like the folks on the northern coast of Colombia. In fact,

Panama was a part of Colombia, before it separated. Another international tourist spot in Panama was the famous Panama Canal. Hundreds of merchant ships and touristic luxury liners pass through it every day. The Panama Canal never sleeps! There are several "Lock Gates" to adjust the differential water levels between the Atlantic and the Pacific oceans, and it takes several hours to bring them on the same level so that the boats can pass. I remember that during our "technical exhibition" at Jadavpur University in Kolkata, India, our group of four students made a working model of the Panama Canal's Lock Gate mechanism. It was indeed a working model, and we exhibited the mechanism to explain to the visitors how the water levels were moved up and down for the boats to pass. We even had the small "toy boats" to show passing through the lock gates, as well as the mechanism of opening and closing the gates. It was a hundred percent working model. Only there were no real tourists on the toy boats. We put some "plastic passengers" of the size of Legos!

Seeing the same "real" gates opening and closing at the *Gatum Gate* in Panama Canal was indeed very exciting for me. I got emotional seeing it working right in front of my eyes that I modeled in 1959 during my third year in Mechanical Engineering undergraduate program. I explained the whole history to Matty and hearing my story of my technical exhibition some fifty years ago, it made her emotional too. That evening we went to a romantic candle-light dinner for celebrating my opening exhibition of a working model of the lock gates of the Panama Canal that happened half a century ago!

We saw passenger boats full of tourists slowly passing through the locks and the tourists from the boats waving friendly hands to us from the deck, and we were just looking at them and sometimes responding to their greetings. It was kind of a one-way treat. So, Matty and I wanted to have a boat ride through Panama Canal and to feel the same way as the tourists on board were enjoying. So, after going back to our hotel we contacted the travel agent and the agent arranged a ride for us, boarding a ship at one end of the canal and disembarking at the other end, thus passing through all the eight lock gates. It was wonderful! We shared the feelings of the tourists from both sides, those who were on-board and the others on the dock. It was a memorable journey through all the lock-gates and get out at the other end. This adventure took eight hours since at each lock people were boarding the boats and getting down.

In February 2020, the problem of Coronavirus COVID-19 spread in Puerto Rico, and all our travel plans had to stop, both internationally as well as in USA. Besides sightseeing and vacation trips, I had two professional travels, one in USA and the other in Europe. This year the ASEE (American Society for Engineering Education) Convention is taking place in- presence (not virtually!) in Minneapolis, MN in late June, and we have a paper selected to present there. In the last week of June there is another technical conference, M2D2022 (Materials for Mechanical Design and Manufacturing) International Conference in the charming island of Madeira, Portugal. Our ME Department has two papers accepted for presentation there. Besides, we have a family get-together in Canada in late July and early August. Furthermore, Matty has a passion for visiting the tall towers, taking the elevator to the topmost floor, where they usually have a restaurant to eat while enjoying a birds-eye view from the topmost floor of the tallest tower. We had done it before many times in Chicago and Seattle in USA as well as in Niagara Falls and Toronto in

Canada. Now she would like to do the same in Dubai to reach the tallest building in the world so far, *Burj Khalifa*! From Dubai to Kolkata, India, there is a two and half hour straight, non-stop flight, and Kolkata is my hometown! Thus, I'd also like to take advantage of the Dubai trip for seeing my sisters and cousins in India. But all such elaborate travel plans in 2022 and thereafter, will depend on how the *Omicron* virus, a new cousin of COVID-19, will behave. It is already doing disasters in Hong Kong and in South-East China, attacking thousands of people, and killing dozens of them.

POSTSCRIPT

My best education, as I remember, began before entering primary school in Grade 3. My mom did my homeschooling from kindergarten and also for the first two grades, starting my informal education when I was only four years old. There was no fixed time schedule. Mother used to sit down with me whenever she had time, mostly after our breakfast (before she started her own daily routine of cooking, house-cleaning, washing our clothes, etc.) or even better, after her little afternoon nap. She would sit with me and teach how to hold a white chalk and write A, B, C on a small black slate. Sometimes we would sing a song together. Then she started training me in reading. Thus, I learned first how to write the English and Bengali alphabets before reading them. This would probably be quite the opposite in a formal school: first read and then write what you read. My mom taught me differently.

There were times when she used to sit with me in the evening or at sunset, after finishing house-spousing and taking her long and most relaxing once-a-day bath. I would sit very close to her with the intention of smelling her body just after bath, washed and perfumed with sandalwood soap! She would teach me how to count, softly singing the multiplication table in Bengali. I still remember and relish the joy of that learning! From Primary School to PhD, I never felt that freedom of learning until I came to Cuernavaca, Mexico in January 1970. Ivan Illich was giving his lecture on Cultural Anthropology, himself sitting under the shade of a huge mango tree, and we, around 10 or 12 of his students, were sitting around him in the most relaxed natural surroundings. I'll never forget that freedom of learning either! Liberty of mind narrowed the gap between a kindergarten kid and a Postdoctoral fellow.

Both the scenes, my mother homeschooling me in her kitchen and Ivan Illich lecturing under a mango tree, had full freedom. They reminded me of Rabindranath Tagore's university *Biswabharati* in Shantiniketan where the students were exposed to that freedom of learning under the canopy of an eternally blue sky. Was it the same scene in Ancient India when Valmiki Muni used to teach *Ramayana* to his disciples, or Guru Patanjali used to recite his *Sutras* to the students in a most natural surrounding under the pine trees? Our education, from Primary School to Postdoctoral Research, needs that liberty of thought, the freedom of our mind!

LAS SEMBLANAZAS

Dr. Jayanta Kumar Banerjee is a professor in Mechanical Engineering Department at the University of Puerto Rico in Mayagüez (UPRM) and a Life Member of the American Society for Engineering Education (ASEE). Apart from engineering, he has written nine books, both poems and essays in English and Spanish. Besides, some of his poems appear in different anthologies published in Argentina, Dominican Republic and Puerto Rico. This book, written in a biographical format, sums up his personal and professional experience.

Carlos A.F. Zapata is a Puerto Rico-based illustrator. Under his art alias, "CafzkaSoft", his illustration work includes character art for video games, videos as well as cover art in both 2D and 3D mediums. He has a BS in Electrical Engineering and is currently pursuing a BS in Digital Animation Sciences.

CPSIA information can be obtained
at www.ICGtesting.com
Printed in the USA
LVHW030634230223
740173LV00002B/11